SECRETS OF THE STREET

SECRETS OF THE STREET

The Dark Side of Making Money

Gene G. Marcial

McGraw-Hill, Inc.

New York   San Francisco   Washington, D.C.   Auckland   Bogotá
Caracas   Lisbon   London   Madrid   Mexico City   Milan
Montreal   New Delhi   San Juan   Singapore
Sydney   Tokyo   Toronto

Library of Congress Cataloging-in-Publication Data

Marcial, Gene G.
    Secrets of the street : the dark side of making money / Gene G.
    Marcial.
       p.   cm.
      ISBN 0-07-040255-8
      1. Wall Street.   2. Insider trading in securities—United States.
    I. Title.
    HG4572.M28   1995
    364.1'68.—dc20   94-42557
                                                 CIP

1 2 3 4 5 6 7 8 9 0   DOH/DOH   9 0 9 8 7 6 5 4

ISBN 0-07-040255-8

Printed and bound by R. R. Donnelley & Sons Company.

For my mother,
Consuelo Generoso-Inayan,
and my daughters,
and to the memory of my son, Generoso.

CONTENTS

PREFACE

A book that focuses on insider trading, by its very essence, can't identify many of the characters involved, nor can it reveal very precise descriptions of events or situations that could uncover my sources. So the names of most of the people as well as companies have been disguised through the use of pseudonyms. In some cases, I had to alter the description of a character's background to honor my promise of confidentiality to my sources. I did similar profile alterations on some of the companies and stocks mentioned. Most of the disguised players in this book are deep insiders who have much to hide—and too much to lose—if their real identities are revealed.

But this book is about *real* people and *real* events. While I have altered many names of the characters and their companies in this book, the events *did* take place and are in fact very accurate representations of what goes on on Wall Street every day of the week.

As a practical matter, I have identified all pseudonyms of people and companies by quotation marks when they are first referenced. All other names not enclosed by quotes are therefore of the actual people or companies.

I'm deeply grateful to a number of personal friends, professional supporters, and otherwise invaluable sources who have made it possible for me to organize and write this book.

I would like to make particular mention of my editor and publisher, Philip Ruppel, and Laura Friedman, also at McGraw-Hill, for their expert advice, professional assistance, and guidance. And special thanks to my research associates, Karla Strom and Jamie Marcial.

Of those who encouraged me to write this book, I am especially indebted to my wife, Kristi Marcial, who has been most inspiring and among the most enthusiastic and supportive of this project.

GENE G. MARCIAL
New York City

The love of money is the root of all evil
1 TIMOTHY 6:10

The Oldest Game

D on't kid yourself: Very little has changed on Wall Street. Half a dozen years after the scandals of the 1980s, when any number of Street veterans were charged with violations of securities laws and several high-profile insiders were marched off to jail, insider trading and market manipulation—in most cases 100 percent illegal—are *still* the most zealously desired play in the financial world. It's almost the only way to make the truly big bucks. All the market savvy in the world will come up short if you're playing against other investors who have market savvy *plus* inside information. Sorry, but that's the way the game is played.

I have worked on Wall Street for over twenty years, the last thirteen of them writing the "Inside Wall Street" column for *Business Week*. I can report that some of the most highly respected and intelligent men and women I have met during those two decades trade in inside information. Are all their activities illegal? No. Many of these activities lie in the broad gray area of the law. But do these investors even need to *risk* breaking the law in order to make a nice living? Hardly. Do they need to risk breaking the law in order to become wealthy? Hardly; many of them are already filthy rich. Are these people otherwise upstanding citizens? As far as I know.

So why do they do it? Because shady and semi-shady trading is part of the culture on Wall Street. But this is nothing new. It certainly didn't start with the now infamous era ushered in by Ronald Reagan. It has always been this way. Consider the following story from seventy years ago.

At the pinnacle of his prestige in the 1920s the legendary J. P. Morgan was nearly as powerful as the President of the United States. He was also the consummate inside trader. Among the bank of telephones on his desk was one hooked directly to the telephone of the chairman of U.S. Steel. This was back when U.S. Steel strode across the industrial landscape like a behemoth.

James C. Sargent, a veteran securities lawyer and a commissioner of the Securities and Exchange Commission (SEC) from 1956 to 1960, tells the following story about the kinds of uses to which that phone link was put. One day Morgan called up the chairman of U.S. Steel and informed him that the company's progress and top line and bottom line and every other line looked terrific.

"Since the company is performing so well and has the money to disburse, why don't you raise your dividend?" Morgan asked. (I paraphrase, of course.)

That sounded like an excellent idea to the chairman. For one thing, Morgan was correct about the facts: The company was going great. For another, a question of that nature from Morgan, whose bank had financed practically all of this country's leading corporations, including U.S. Steel, was more on the order of a command.

After receiving this very positive response from the steel chieftain, as expected, Morgan quickly picked up one of the other phones and called some of his more valued clients. His message was clear enough: Buy shares of U.S. Steel. (If his advice to the U.S. Steel chairman had been to cut the dividend, as it had been at times, his message to those clients would have been to sell the stock.)

Morgan's "suggestion" to the chairman and the chairman's positive response constituted knowledge of an impending hike in the dividend; Morgan then informed his clients of that hike before the information was made public. Under today's laws and court rulings this is nothing more or less than insider trading, and it is illegal. This is the definition of insider trading: buying and selling stocks on the basis of material information not available to the investing public.

In those good old days, however, there was little regard for insider trading or conflicts of interest among investors and CEOs and other insiders because there were hardly any laws regulating the flow and use of inside information. Now there are reams of regulations designed to identify, thwart, and, if necessary, prosecute the dozens of infractions known generically as insider trading. But no matter. These are the good old days too. Insider manipulations are just about as rampant today as they were in Morgan's heyday. Who's counting?

Another, more recent J. P. Morgan story dates from 1990, when an officer at the top-of-the-line investment bank that bears that venerable name was charged with insider trading. This was Rushton Ardrey, a senior vice president of J. P. Morgan and Co. and also a director of the wholly owned subsidiary, Morgan Capital Corp.

One day, James Morgan, an asset manager at Morgan Capital who reported directly to Ardrey (and no relationship to the J. P. Morgan family), confided to his boss that the management at one of the bank's clients, LPL Technologies, was preparing a management-led leveraged buyout (LBO) of LPL. Morgan knew about the proposed LBO because he was responsible for monitoring Morgan Capital's investment in LPL Technologies and had been consulted about the proposed deal.

Of course, this information was top-notch "material, nonpublic information." But that didn't deter Rushton Ardrey from buying shares of LPL as quietly as possible—in other words, in small increments. By the time LPL announced on March 19, 1990, that it had received a tender offer from management, Ardrey had accumulated 18,000 shares. After the announcement the stock rose, naturally, and a month later Ardrey sold his shares for a profit of $129,586, according to the SEC, which was tipped off about the case. Apparently Ardrey had in-house enemies. Eventually he agreed without admitting or denying the charges to a consent order permanently barring him from working in the securities industry and requiring him to pay back the

$129,586. (James Morgan was not prosecuted because passing along the information about the LPL buyout to Rushton was part of his job. Ardrey was the one who traded in the information and therefore broke the law.)

For every Rushton Ardrey caught with his hand in the insiders' till, how many of the Streetwise who trade in illicit information walk away unscathed with their profits? No one can be sure. Dozens, certainly, as we shall see. Hundreds, maybe, if you include all those who operate in the gray area of the law. And hundreds, definitely, if you include the traders who scam the public with perfectly *legal* means. As we shall also see.

Ardrey was exposed in 1990, but the issue of insider trading, market manipulation, junk bonds, and all the rest— the image of Wall Street as a culture of unalloyed greed— had already come to a head in 1986. Ardrey was back-page stuff, while the arrest and subsequent conviction in 1987 of arbitrageur Ivan Boesky and some of his closest friends and associates was front-page news, evening news news. Boesky's involvement took the issue of insider trading to the highest and most visible levels of Wall Street, finally culminating in the arrest of Michael Milken. No longer could malfeasance be laid at the feet of a few renegade young Turks operating "on their own." It turned out that the young Turks had learned at the knees of the *old* Turks. It turned out that if you weren't a Turk on Wall Street, you were a turkey, an outsider trying to play an insider's game.

The system itself was in the docket. After the Securities and Exchange Commission moved in on Boesky, he said, "I know that in the wake of today's events, many will call for reforms. If any mistakes launch a process of reexamination of the rules and practices of our financial marketplace, then perhaps some good will result."

The premise of this book is that eight years after that scandal, despite a thorough "reexamination of the rules and practices" of Wall Street, it's still business as usual for Wall Street insiders. Unethical and sometimes illegal insider trading abounds. It happens daily, hourly, every minute of every day, and sometimes on Sunday too.

Remember, men and women don't work on Wall Street to make the world safe for democracy and capitalism. If those venerable institutions happen to benefit from the collective efforts of the Wall Street wizards, that's good, but it's not the main point. People work on Wall Street in order to make as much money as possible in the shortest period of time.

Now, add to this basic motivation the fact that Wall Street is a beehive of secret intelligence or maybe a Garden of Eden lush with secrets. You don't have to be an Ivan Boesky or a Michael Milken to get your hands on some of the good stuff. As the cliché goes, "It's easy when you know how." It's easy when you're connected. It's easy when you've helped someone else with a well-timed tip to receive another one in return. It's easy when there are so many companies and so much information and so many people and so much sheer greed.

Common sense dictates that insider trading of one variety or another (there are hundreds of varieties, legal and illegal) will be the order of the day whenever possible.

Perfect Information

As it turns out, Ivan Boesky had been one of the most reliable sources for journalists for quite a few years. If a reporter received a tip that, say, CBS shares were being accumulated for a possible buyout deal, Boesky was one of the first Wall Streeters he or she would call to check out the rumor. He was uncanny at analyzing how the pattern of trading in a company's stock could reveal a takeover play that was pending or already in the works. Usually he could give a capsule profile of the cast of characters involved. As the king of the arbitrageurs, Boesky was a fountain of information—when he wanted to be.

Of course, when I heard the news of his arrest, I immediately understood *why* he had had such an uncanny knowledge of the deepest secrets on the Street. I had never suspected that he had been engaged in bribery to obtain some of his information. Maybe I should have been suspicious because so often his information wasn't merely good, it was *perfect*. And perfect information has a tendency to be illegal.

The term "perfect information" was first brought to my attention by investment banker Jeff Beck, known as Mad Dog on the Street because of his maverick style of trading and strange houndlike mannerisms at the trading desk. In the early 1980s, while Boesky and everyone else on the Street were still riding high, Beck said to me in a phone conversation, "Pretty soon things will explode and Boesky will end up in a lot of dog shit. You should expose this bastard. I tell you it will make a great book, and I will help you for sure in proving such cases. He deserves it for using all that perfect information in his dealings."

I like the phrase. It's perfect. Unfortunately, or perhaps, fortunately, I didn't follow through on Beck's proposal to collaborate. He subsequently joined Oppenheimer & Co. as head of its mergers and acquisition unit, where he cottoned up to another *Business Week* writer, Tony Bianco, to write about his exploits. This book mentioned that Beck had been after certain journalists to expose Boesky. In his book, Bianco revealed how Beck went beyond exaggeration into outright fabrication in telling the story of his life.

Beck was just a voice on the phone, but I had met Ivan Boesky. We occasionally enjoyed a drink or a game of squash at the Harvard Club on 44th Street, where he was a member even though he was not a graduate of Harvard, much less a faculty member. In his best-selling book *Den of Thieves*, James Stewart said that Boesky had bought his way into the club by donating a lot of money to one of Harvard's least known graduate schools, the School of Public Health, and had been named to that school's board of overseers. This was the coveted "faculty-level" appointment that also qualified this graduate of the Detroit College of Law for membership in the Harvard Club.

Throughout our casual friendship Boesky had never volunteered a story *per se* for my column. Generally he answered my questions about specific situations. But on one occasion—in fact, just two months before his shocking confession in November 1986—he called me at *Business Week* to say that he had a story for me to consider, but not for attribution. He was mulling the idea of selling the world-famous Beverly Hills Hotel to one of several groups—a major U.S. airline company, a large hotel chain in Tokyo, or one of a couple of U.S. investor groups, including one led by the financier Marvin Davis. I published the story in my column—a modest scoop. Two months later Ivan was arrested—an earthshaking scoop. A few months after that Marvin Davis and his people took the hotel off his troubled hands.

About a year after his arrest and exactly one month after Black Monday—October 19, 1987—Boesky walked into the federal prison in Lompoc, California, to serve twenty-two months of hard time. He then served four months in a halfway house in Brooklyn. For the next six years, in prison and then after his release, Boesky was incommunicado with the outside world. He gave no interviews. For someone whose name had been a fixture of the news broadcasts as the convicted king of the arbs, he was remarkably successful in disappearing from the public eye. I was therefore more than a little surprised when he returned my phone call in June 1993 from his home in La Jolla, California.

We had not seen each other or spoken in about seven years. My world had been more or less the same in the interim, while his had changed beyond all recognition—or had it? I wanted to find out, and he agreed to let me.

We met two months later, in October 1993, in the bar and lounge of the Peninsula Hotel on 55th Street in Manhattan. Now fifty-seven years old, he looked strikingly dapper in his dark blue Armani suit, white silk shirt, Versace tie, and neatly trimmed shoulder-length white hair— a far cry from the ex-con photographed leaving prison on a furlough in 1990. That man had looked like a latter-day Howard Hughes. This new incarnation of Ivan Boesky was suave, urbane, and totally self-assured. His eyes were as piercing and full of curiosity as they had been during the years of triumph. My first thought in the Peninsula Hotel was that this was not a man in the throes of any kind of continuing crisis—financial, legal, or "existential"—and Ivan immediately confirmed that impression.

"I'm enjoying my anonymity and 'nonexistence' in the media for a change," he said with a smile early in our conversation. He made a point of distinguishing between himself and Michael Milken, who went to prison partly as a result of the testimony of Boesky. "I wouldn't parade myself on television like Milken does, insisting that he has never made a dirty dollar. That's ridiculous. A load of crap."

Beyond that remark, Boesky would not talk about the other main players on the Street back in the 1980s.

I have to admit that I was curious about Boesky's day-to-day life in prison, mainly because I knew that prior to prison he had been a remarkably fastidious man. According to his ex-wife, Seema (they had gone through a bitter divorce following his release), he instructed his children not to flush the toilet: That chore was properly the household help's. This was a man who—again according to Seema—wanted his very special, perfectly warmed salmon dinner the moment he arrived home from work at their luxurious $10 million mansion in Westchester County north of New York City. For him to be served this dinner, five or six salmon steaks were placed in the oven at ten-minute intervals. One of them would be perfect when Boesky sat down at the table. I asked Boesky to comment about this, but he declined to discuss any details.

What goes around comes around. I felt certain that Boesky had to flush his own toilet in prison. I felt certain that to eat at all, he would have had to do so when the warden said so, and with good odds that the ground round was overcooked.

But I did not receive confirmation. He would not speak of life in prison, not surprising in a man who had been at the pinnacle of his career one of the most influential and sought after market gurus on Wall Street, a scourge of corporate America who had at his command more than $3 billion in cash to employ in takeover raids. Such a man is not likely to spend a lot of time looking *back*, especially back at prison.

What books had he read? What thoughts had occupied his mind? Boesky pushed the questions aside. "People know me as an ex-convict, a fellow who went to jail," he explained.

"If I focused on that event in my life, I would be perpetuating that image of myself as a jailbird. I would be sending myself back to prison one more time."

He would speak only of life after prison, and that life, he assured me, was excellent. In that life he can once again enjoy his very special, perfectly warmed salmon dinner the moment he desires it.

"An absolutely happy life!" he exclaimed. "I am comfortable and quite content, believe it or not. The most valuable—extremely important—thing I have now is freedom. And I'm not just talking about my being out of prison. But at this point of my life I am free to do anything that I want to do. I am a free man, Gene. I can invest and buy or sell anything, like everybody else. It is true that I can't be a broker-dealer or manage money for others for a fee. I am specifically barred from accepting any fee when providing investment advice or services. But if I wanted to give advice for free on, say, buying IBM, I most certainly could do that."

Although Ivan is indeed free to manage and invest his own money in the United States, his assets and major investments, including the funds that were not seized by the government when he was arrested, are stashed away somewhere overseas, according to one of his old Street friends. This man says, "Any money he now has is definitely outside the reach of the U.S. authorities, for obvious reasons. One reason is to avoid any entanglements with the Internal Revenue Service."

Another Street trader who's aware of Boesky's current activities claims that he is now the brains behind, and the real owner of, a $1 billion fund in the Netherlands Antilles, with about two-thirds of that money being Boesky's own. Officially, though, the fund is owned, this source claims, by a foreign corporation headed by a different individual.

One persistent Wall Street story contends that Boesky's much publicized divorce from Seema was a put-up job, even though his claim for alimony and the publicly expressed bitter insults between Ivan and Seema were savored by the tabloids and the national press. Such embarrassing (and predictable) coverage would seem to be a high price to pay for a scam, but Boesky's critics are insistent. They allege that the alimony Ivan won—$20 million in cash, a $2.5 million home, and $180,000 a year—was an engineered move that enabled him to spend legitimately the millions in cash he had entrusted to Seema for safekeeping in addition to the wads stashed in numbered accounts in Switzerland and the Netherlands Antilles.

Seated in the bar of the Peninsula Hotel sipping an espresso, Boesky declined to comment on any such reports regarding his finances or his divorce.

"Boesky is very much in touch with his old buddies on Wall Street too, which is not an illegal thing for him to do," adds one of his peers. In fact, this man says that Boesky is a big customer of some of his former colleagues, since his fund in the Netherlands Antilles invests and trades heavily in American securities. If this is correct, his old trading pals are probably excited about Boesky's return to the business. These people stand to benefit from his trading skills and stock-picking savvy. He has made a lot of money for other people over the years. They're not likely to turn around and discredit him.

"As long as Boesky's operations remain quiet, low-profile, and 'legal,'" says one former associate, "they would love doing business with the old fox."

There's also another consideration: Boesky got caught. Many others on Wall Street—while not dealing in as much money as Boesky, granted—get away with insider trading every day, and the Street knows it.

Boesky and I met for a second round of drinks at the Peninsula on April 1, 1994, just about the time when the market had retreated by nearly 10 percent from its historic high earlier in the year. The retreat followed a short-term rise in interest rates by the Federal Reserve Board, and most investors assumed that the outlook for interest rates was higher still. And they were right. Three weeks after Boesky's and my second conversation the Fed nudged up the rates for the third time in 1994. Investors were deeply worried about the stock market's direction.

Boesky, however, was bullish on stocks. "I am fairly optimistic about the market, and I think it is presenting investors with a lot of opportunities to buy stocks cheaply again," he said. He disagreed with the notion of the Fed's chairman, Alan Greenspan, that inflation has to be conquered effectively by raising interest rates very early in the cycle: "From what I have seen, there should be little concern about inflation, so the Fed's move was really premature."

Make no mistake: Ivan Boesky is alive and well in the stock-picking business. The hotel business has also caught his fancy. In his heyday he had owned the Beverly Hills Hotel. Now his interest was piqued by a report that the legendary Hotel Bel-Air was expected to be put up for sale in Los Angeles. Boesky had tried to buy that hotel when he and Seema had owned the Beverly Hills, but his offer of $27 million had been bested by the oil heiress Caroline Hunt's offer of $36 million. Two years later Ms. Hunt turned around and sold the posh property to a Japanese group for $110 million. Now they may sell the place.

If so, Boesky may be in for disappointment a second time because other moneyed bidders, including Hollywood music mogul David Geffen, the Los Angeles-based real estate investment firm Colony Capital Inc., and perhaps the Sultan of Brunei (who bought the Beverly Hills Hotel from Marvin Davis), are also eyeing the property.

As the time approached 5 P.M., the thickly carpeted Peninsula lounge began filling up, and this in-the-know New York crowd definitely knew Ivan Boesky's profile. Even if they did not know who he was, curious glances were directed at his deep tan, flowing white hair, and sartorial elegance. But most of the other drinkers and diners knew who he was, and their stares were not just curious. They were looks of disapproval, even hostility. During the time we spent in the lounge I didn't sense any sign of friendly recognition or sympathy. So this was not a Wall Street crowd. At best, these people allowed us a polite distance while giving Ivan a momentary cold stare. Ivan seemed impervious to the attention, but the idea that he was at one time public enemy number one was not lost on him at all. In fact, I sensed that if there was one thing bothering Boesky about the whole affair seven years earlier, it was this disturbing idea that the entire nation has turned against him.

"I know I violated the law," he stressed to me more than once. "I've paid my debt to society." As far as he's concerned, his case is over: "That's all done with and behind me now. There are no more lawsuits—none are pending. They've all been settled. So it's time for me to move on."

It is an understandable wish.

"I feel I have gained more than I have lost. I'm at peace within myself. My priorities in life have changed. I feel wonderful, really. I'm now surrounded by my real friends, I have a pleasant time of it, and things are good," claimed the man who disrupted not only many aspects of the way Wall Street operates but also the lives of many investors and their families who were embroiled in one of the biggest financial scandals in American history.

Boesky also said, "Not everything is about money now."

What kind of remorse does he feel? He said he is honestly sorry for his trangressions. But he thinks his punishment was more than adequate, including the $100 million fine he paid.

What is his "explanation" for his crimes? Ivan tried to deflect the question. When I suggested that his name was now forever linked with the greed mania of the 1980s, he did say, "It was not just a matter of money or greed. There were many other reasons, other factors on why things happened the way they did, and why I did what I did. It wasn't all that simple."

He declined to say in hindsight whether he had done the right thing in agreeing early to a negotiated guilty plea. Some legal experts assert that Boesky made a grievous tactical legal error when he did so. If he had stood his ground and battled U.S. Attorney Rudy Giuliani (now the mayor of New York City) to the end, the results might have been different, they say. But again, this is a question from the past on which Boesky does not intend to dwell.

He asked me rhetorically, "What about those other years when I was functioning as a positive and productive citizen and a humane person? I didn't start just recently being nice to children and hugging them and donating money for their welfare. I had done work for charities, contributing funds for various causes early on in my career—and long before I had gone astray."

So there is some rancor toward the media, which he believes conspired to give him the ultimate bad rap. He insisted that nobody bothered to "balance things" with what was happening elsewhere (and everywhere) on Wall Street at the time. He would like people to see him in the context of the pernicious and negative circumstances that plagued the financial markets during the 1980s. In effect, he argues, he was just one of the many who were swept away by this giant storm of corruption, greed, and decadence and one of the few who were caught.

As he rose to signal an end to our discussion, Boesky said it was wonderful that his new life has allowed him to spend a lot of time with his children. His son Bill Boesky, a writer and playwright, premiered his new rock musical,

Fallen Angel, in April at the off-Broadway Circle in the Square Theatre. In part, the play deals with how the author coped with his father's status as a convicted felon. Ivan Boesky attended the opening. His daughter is a law student and his twin sons are in college.

"And now I am going to do something very interesting and very important to me," Boesky concluded as we shook hands. "I am going to St. John the Divine Church in Harlem and attend the Easter mass and listen to Easter music."

The Bagman

van Boesky is out of the picture for now, or at least he's lying low. But there are plenty of pretenders on the Street. Let's now see where these Street insiders obtain their information, when this activity is legal and when it is illegal, who controls the ill-found facts, and how these insiders use them to cash in. Let's see how insider trading and market manipulation—legal and illegal—are built into the infrastructure of the system.

To begin, I introduce a slightly balding seasoned investment adviser by the name "Jack Flaherty." I know this man well, but like many other names in this book, this one is pure invention. By definition, Wall Street insiders want to stay that way—inside—and one of the quickest ways to be shown the door and turned into an outsider is to talk too much. On the record, that is. You can talk all you want off the record, or anonymously.

So Jack Flaherty it is, because Jack is definitely an insider on the Street and wants to stay that way. On this particular early afternoon in March 1991, just as on most early afternoons throughout the year, Jack almost reeks of the heavy odor of the Chivas Regal he acquired over lunch in his usual pair of shots at Delmonico's, right around the corner from his office on Wall Street. Almost daily Jack holds forth at his accustomed table at this famous Street hangout, regaling friend and foe alike (although Jack has very few foes) with opinionated conversation spiced with loud and colorful expletives, arching his full-blown eyebrows, and flashing his impish grin.

Back in his office on this particular afternoon in March he has every right to wag his eyebrows and flash that Jack Nicholson grin. He has just scored big-time. He grabs the phone.

"Hey, Bob, Jack Flaherty here," he gloats. "Was everything to your ... satisfaction?"

Jack roars with pleasure.

The man on the other end of the line is "Bob Cummings," also a pseudonym. Bob is one of the star money managers for "Popular Investments," as I shall call this mutual funds conglomerate. Bob is twenty-five years younger than Jack Flaherty, and he dresses in a manner that intends to prove it: Giorgio Armani all the way, including the latest style in horn-rimmed eyeglasses. Nor is Bob pushing the limits of his budget with his attire. As one of the rising stars at Popular after only four years with the firm, he can afford all the clothes he wants. Bob regularly beats the performance of the

Dow Jones Industrial Average as he manipulates his portion of the many billions in assets handled annually by Popular.

Like a lot of people in his business, Bob is stingy about accepting phone calls. If he talked with everyone trying to tout stocks to him, he wouldn't have time for anything else. As it is, he fields dozens of pitches every day. But he has to take this call from Jack Flaherty. He has been expecting it. He has to concede defeat.

"Yeah, Jack, it was perfectly . . . satisfying," Bob admits. "Only you could pull off that kind of trick. You've managed to drag me down to your level. You win."

Bob has to admit to himself that "it" had been a good deal *more* than perfectly satisfying. In fact, seldom had he enjoyed "losing" as much as he had three hours earlier, when the receptionist had buzzed him with the information that someone was waiting outside to deliver something to him.

"I think you should come out here, Bob," the receptionist said in an ominous tone of voice. "It's supposed to be, um, well, kind of *personal delivery,* I guess." She paused. "Or I could have it brought in."

Bob hesitated. He had a hunch that this "delivery" had something to do with the persistent Jack Flaherty, who had been hounding him for weeks about the allures of a certain biotech company. I will call this company "Medicure." It would be just like Jack to interrupt another morning for him. It was almost eleven o'clock, and Bob had to be at the "21" Club by noon for a "road show" presentation to money managers by a different biotech firm. He wanted to get there early for the preliminary round of drinks, and so Bob was tempted to turn away no matter what was waiting for him in the reception area. But he gave in.

"Send him in," he barked into the speaker phone. "And I'm out of here right after this, okay? Nothing else."

Bob glanced up as the door opened, prepared to accept the package, whatever it was, with a polite but abrupt thank you. But he never got the words out of his mouth. This particular "messenger" was an absolutely stunning woman with long blond hair and a long, *long* body encased—barely—in a tight red miniskirt and matching red blouse. Everybody in the vicinity at Popular Investments had watched as this woman had walked down the hallway to Bob Cummings's corner office. She had the style and flair of a runway model, and Bob couldn't take his eyes off her as she walked into his office, closed the door carefully behind her, and then strode across the carpet toward his desk without saying a word.

Neither of them said a word.

Although Bob may be only in his middle thirties, he knows a thing or two about the way the world works, including the world of Wall Street. But he had never seen anything like this or even heard about anything quite so flagrant. He was utterly speechless as this stunning woman smiled gently, knowingly, and stepped around his desk. Bob made an involuntary move back.

"Please, Bob," she said as she knelt before him.

Before she left, this woman withdrew a business card from the pocket of her blouse, placed it gently on Bob's desk, and murmured, "Jack sends his best."

Bob watched her close the door to his office before glancing at the card. He already knew which of the several Jacks of his acquaintance was responsible for this unique . . . inducement.

Now back in his office after the road show engagement at "21," Bob is on the phone acknowledging defeat to Jack Flaherty. Laughing on the phone with Jack, Bob glances down at the confirmation sheets on his desk.

"I've already told my trading guy to buy the stock, Jack," Bob tells him.

In fact, just minutes after the woman in the red miniskirt had left his office, Bob had called the chief trader at Popular Investments with instructions to buy 400,000 shares of Medicure for the seven mutual funds for which Bob is responsible. Medicure was selling at $10 at the time.

"I'm finally seeing what I like to see in Medicure," he had said to the trader, who knew that Bob had been resisting repeated pitches for Medicure for weeks, maybe months, because he wasn't convinced that the company had exciting prospects. Its main goal during this period was the development of protein-based pharmaceuticals. "The stock looks better at $10. I think I've waited long enough."

And Bob was specific in his instructions to the trader: The stock should be purchased in blocks of 20,000 and 30,000 shares and as quietly as possible so the stock wouldn't blast off and call unnecessary attention to itself. Bob doesn't want that to happen—yet.

On the phone he tells Jack, "You're the devil, my man, know that. But thanks."

Then he asks offhandedly, in the manner of an after-thought, "Tell me, who was she?"

On his end of the line Jack smiles. He knew this was coming. They always want to know.

"Just call me when you need her," Jack replies to Bob.

And so it goes in the life of investment advisers like Jack Flaherty and money managers like Bob Cummings. The episode with the woman in the red miniskirt actually happened, and it really was a red miniskirt. For months Jack had been trying to sell Bob on the attributes of Medicure. He had given Bob's wife a gold bracelet for her birthday. Several analysts from the major brokerage houses had also, but not necessarily coincidentally, been raving to Bob about Medicure. But even though Bob Cummings had remained unconvinced about the stock, Jack Flaherty had not given up. Several decades of experience on Wall Street had taught him that he'd eventually make the big score with Medicure, maybe not with Bob Cummings, maybe with another of the several targets he had picked for the stock, but with somebody.

How could he be so confident? Jack Flaherty is a Wall Street "bagman" nonpareil. The business card may say "Investment Adviser," but on the Street Jack and his peers are just as often referred to as bagmen (even though some of them are women). The financial world is practically choked with these "investment advisers," who are nothing more or less than promoters, hired guns on the "sell side," stock touts who know how to grease the wheels of the Wall Street money machine.

Who hires the bagmen? Companies (that is, top management) that want to promote their stock over a particular time period. Bagmen are also hired by individuals and groups that wish to see their favorite stock fly all the way to the moon—quickly—and believe that they can make a plausible case for that stock.

The best way for management to boost a stock in this manner is to go to where the big money is, that is, to the big individual and, even more important, to the institutional investors. And the best way to get the attention of these movers and shakers on the "buy side" of the market is through an investment adviser like Jack Flaherty, a bagman who knows all the ropes and all the angles and knows how to get through even the heaviest of doors.

Jack's personal "stable" of Wall Street contacts includes money managers like Bob Cummings, brokers, institutional salespersons, analysts, traders, and even a sprinkling of influential contacts within the government—city, state, and federal. Jack has to be prepared for all eventualities, and he is. That's why he's practically assured of success whenever he launches a campaign. Nor does he have to wait long. A zealous campaign by Jack or any other top bagman will often start to bear fruit within a month and will almost always succeed within three months.

The slang term used for these operators refers to the practically bottomless bag of gifts—cash, drugs, jewelry, cars, and, of course, women—that top bagmen have at their disposal. They are prodigious entertainers who think nothing of throwing yacht parties or escorting important investors on an evening's tour of Manhattan's toniest restaurants and clubs. One of Jack's favorite stops on these jaunts is Stringfellows on 20th Street in Manhattan, a neon and chrome disco in which the clothing of the employees, such as it is, is held up with ... strings.

The woman in Bob Cummings's office? She was an employee at Stringfellows, and she often leaves the shop after an evening's work with $1,000 in small bills slipped inside her bikini. Flaherty is in the habit of getting his guests into the spirit of the party at Stringfellows by providing them with a ready supply of twenty-dollar bills with which to tip the entertainers. It's nothing for Jack to drop several thousand on this type of diversion in one evening.

He says quite frankly, "These places are among the best business meeting rooms to close deals in."

No expense is spared by a veteran bagman, who can well afford to bestow these gifts because the rewards reaped by the best are enormous. Jack Flaherty estimates he has grossed about $10 million in the last four years, an income that mocks the comparative chump change he made while working for many years as a stockbroker and then as a trader on the Street.

The major payment a bagman receives from a company he or she has agreed to tout is shares of stock, either gratis or purchased at a deep discount. This arrangement gives the bagman an extra inducement to produce results. In addition, the bagman often purchases shares over and above those he or she has been tendered up-front.

Small companies going public with an initial public offering (IPO) are the mother lode of stock bonanzas for bagmen. By definition, these companies are looked at with caution by the big institutional investors. The best way for management to overcome these justified concerns is through the services of a bagman. You can rest assured that a small company embarking on an IPO will hire the best bagman it can afford. In this situation the investment adviser has all the leverage. The company in question will not have a lot of cash on hand, but the bagman will fill up with free or discounted shares. A bagman like Jack Flaherty will make twice the fee from a small, emerging company that he would earn from a large company. From Medicure he earned a $100,000 fee for three months' work, plus warrants to buy a large number of shares at discount.

In fact, prominent companies have no need for an independent bagman. Their stock is widely known; its attributes are widely known. These companies get along fine with an in-house promoter known as the investor relations officer. This individual works hand in hand with outside public relations flacks to push the stock. This New York–based PR firm will do some of the same things Jack Flaherty does, but it will *not* hand out the lavish gifts. Parties, yes. Diamond bracelets, no. And certainly no stunning women in tight red miniskirts dispatched to one's office at 11 A.M.

But freelance bagmen have no such compunctions. Without exception, they are smart, articulate talkers who will do what's necessary to bag a targeted money manager or large investor. And there is no doubt whatsoever that among the resources at their disposal, buried deeply or not so deeply in their trusty bag of goodies, is inside information. When a company solicits the services of a bagman, the chief executive officer supplies him or her with as much information as possible, sometimes including "insidy" information, in order to whet his or her appetite for the project.

Inevitably, therefore, the bagman becomes a conduit for the passing of inside information, working both sides of the fence. From the CEO or perhaps chief financial officer on one side, he or she acquires real information about the company at stake. From the investors and money managers on the other side, he or she acquires *relationships* that pay off in the form of future information regarding other stocks and other deals. A classic piece of inside information is an impending large purchase (or sale) by a major money manager. A trusted bagman may be tipped off about this transaction.

This kind of cross-pollination gives the "investment adviser" a network that provides almost unparalleled inside information. The biggest bonanza of all for the bagmen results from trading on this inside information for their own accounts.

How do they swing this? Let's return to Jack Flaherty's office immediately after he concludes his conversation with Bob Cummings, who has just acknowledged purchasing

400,000 shares of Medicure at around $10. Jack buzzes "Vivian," his secretary of long standing.

"Vivian, we got it!" Jack exclaims. "Now, Viv, go to it. And play it cool, know what I mean? But fast."

He can't resist one final display of victory, jumping from his leather swivel chair, punching the air with his fist, and almost shouting, "Yes! Mr. Clean finally came through."

For her part, Vivian immediately gets her friend "Jon" on the line. Jon is a trader whom Vivian has dated a couple of times. In the special voice she uses for just such occasions— the throaty voice that sounds as if it were divulging major military secrets in the middle of the cold war—she whispers, "Jon, a big block of Medicure will be trading shortly. Popular Investments is buying."

Jon replies in the slight affected accent he retains after ten years in America, "Dahling, I owe you three elegant dinners."

At least three. Jon is delighted with the news. The move by Popular almost guarantees some kind of tick upward for Medicure stock. This is a no-brainer. Jon immediately places several buy orders with his traders. Some of these purchases are for his "discretionary" customers, for whom he can buy and sell without consultation (they sign a contract to this effect), and some are for his personal portfolio.

Meanwhile, Vivian is back on the phone, this time with "David" over at another brokerage house. David has been Vivian's drinking buddy for ten years.

Same voice, same story: "Medicure will move big, and you guys'd better jump onto the wagon *muy rapido*." Vivian picked up a little Spanish on a recent trip to Mexico City, and these two words also come through loud and clear on Wall Street.

No sooner does David put down the phone than the tape displays two blocks of 30,000 shares of Medicure trading at $10⅛. This is followed shortly by a group of blocks, 4,000 and 5,000 shares apiece, for a total of 55,000 shares. (This was Jon's order moments before.)

Now the Medicure cat is really out of the bag. Traders all over town—all over the country—wake up to what's happening in Medicure. By the closing bell at 4 P.M., the stock has recorded a 30 percent hike, from $10 to $13—a big score for any stock, and a really big score for one that has been as sleepy as long as Medicure has.

Conjecture swirls. The wire services and other business reporters call their most trusted sources on the Street, including analysts. The Dow Jones news wire calls the company directly. By the following day, while block trades of Medicure continue to sprint across the tape, speculation focuses on a possible announcement by the Food and Drug Administration regarding positive results concerning one of Medicure's products then undergoing clinical trials. *USA Today* financial correspondent Dan Dorfman (since moved to *Money* magazine) mentions the excitement over Medicure on his midday broadcast on the CNBC cable network. He refers to the buying by some mutual fund managers as unusually strong. Dorfman rattles off analysts' earning estimates and bullish ratings for Medicure.

"My sources tell me they expect the stock to climb to higher levels," Dorfman says in his incomparably raspy and strained voice. "But they could be wrong. Who knows?"

Dorfman is well aware that rumors about biotech companies are a dime a dozen. By this point he's suspicious about all of them, and he has every right to be. Arguably the most popular and controversial of all the financial writers and broadcasters (and perhaps the highest paid as well), Dorfman has been dead right many times while reporting on takeovers and other "exclusive" corporate developments, but he doesn't want to go all the way out on a limb on this Medicure development. (By the way, this story about Medicure is an instance that contradicts the criticism sometimes leveled at Dorfman that he is a "friend of the shorts" who specialize in dumping on companies and their stocks. It's not true. One reason for the criticism might be that the shorts are nasty enemies when one publishes or broadcasts a bullish report on a company they have shorted. Like Dorfman, I know all about this. When you read criticism of financial writers, you definitely have to consider the source.)

As it turns out, Dorfman could have gone out on a limb with Medicure. Within weeks the stock was trading at $20. In the next five months the stock would double to $40. And by the end of 1991 the stock would be up to $63, a red-hot winner. But by that time Jack Flaherty and his happy band of "conspirators," including several veteran brokers who knew that Jack was touting Medicure, were long gone from the stock. These insiders had been quietly acquiring Medicure for months before Jack's campaign was officially launched. Within weeks of Bob Cummings's purchase of the 400,000 shares for Popular, the group cashed in with a gross profit of $10 million. And Jack's loyal secretary and fellow tout Vivian received a nice reward.

Of course, Bob Cummings also scored big in his first "deal" with Jack Flaherty. Bob subsequently became a regular participant in the veteran bagman's operations. For Jack himself, who already had all the money he could spend, the Medicure coup was just another in a long series of thrills and deals. This was an orchestrated manipulation of a stock, including outright bribery in the process of touting a stock. It was also a misuse of nonpublic information, specifically the impending massive purchase of shares by Popular Investments. Nevertheless, Jack contends that this episode concerning Medicure is standard operating procedure on the Street, and who's to disagree? Jack is not concerned about ethical issues.

He told me bluntly, "Everybody's doing the same thing. Call it insider trading if you like. Who cares? Nobody gets hurt; that's the important thing."

Perhaps, but that's irrelevant. The important point about this kind of insider trading is not who does or does not get hurt but rather who does or does not have an equal opportunity to *benefit*, especially in the earliest stages of the campaign. Jack's operations demonstrate how uneven the playing field—the stock market—actually is. They are a classic demonstration of the value of inside information. Besides, people *do* get hurt financially. Before Jack's involvement Medicure was behaving in a very ho-hum manner. As a result of the manipulations orchestrated by Jack, average investors ended up paying a higher price for their shares. The stock would not have performed as it did without Jack's manipulations.

Not every investor—in fact, very few investors—have the opportunity to acquire the kind of information that leads to, in Jack's case, a fine home in Westchester County north of Manhattan, a luxurious New York City apartment purchased for $2 million in the rip-roaring 1980s, a Rolls-Royce, and a run-of-the-mill Mercedes-Benz. But these caveats don't deter Jack Flaherty. "Bagman" may sound to the outsider like a lowly profession, but Jack the ultimate insider revels in the description. He's not about to retire in glory and enjoy life in Florida by the side of his wife of many years. Not Jack. He's already signed his next company. He picks up the phone.

"Hey, Steve! Jack here. How ya been, buddy? Say, have you heard about . . . ?"

And if these everyday blandishments don't work . . . .

The Gatekeepers

ob Cummings's business card says "Investment Manager" because this has the ring of integrity about it, but the term I've always preferred for Bob's job is "money manager," because this has the ring of *truth*.

Bob manages money—other people's money. It couldn't be simpler. He and the herd of other money managers on the Street invest the enormous sums accumulated by insurance companies, corporate pension funds, mutual funds, hedge funds, foundations, and the army of portfolio managers who can step to the plate in this billion-dollar league.

While the bagman Jack Flaherty and his cohorts on the sell side of the market cash in time and again, as we have seen, as a general rule they can do so only by going through Bob Cummings and other money managers on the buy side. The reason is simple: Bob and company control the big money that buys the big blocks of stock that drive the big

swings on the Big Board. All the 100-share blocks in the
world will not budge the price of IBM. (A little exaggeration, but not much.) However, that one order from Bob
Cummings for 400,000 shares of Medicure, even though it
was broken by the trader into smaller blocks, was the cata-
lyst for that infamous get-rich-quick caper.

The money managers are the gatekeepers. One way or
another almost every scheme for making millions on Wall
Street requires their cooperation. It follows that money
managers are among the most richly rewarded laborers on
the Street. These men and women are high atop the money
heap, looking back down at the rest of us. They have carte
blanche in terms of investing their clients' wealth, and they
are practically licensed to make a killing for themselves
while doing so.

If a manager is worth his or her salt, he or she will
make lots of money without any kind of shenanigans. It's
done every day. Information is the coin of the realm in
investment, and collecting this information about any and
every detail of corporate and political life is the job of
money managers. It's their raison d'être, if you will. These
men and women are the necessary recyclers of fact and
speculation. They draw vital conclusions from these raw
facts and data. The wheels of commerce—at least on Wall
Street—would grind to a halt without them. This is as it
should be.

At the same time, it is very hard for money managers to
resist taking advantage of the most valuable tool at their disposal: *inside* information. Good, solid public information

may be the coin of the realm, but inside information is pure gold, money in the bank. And nobody but nobody is more likely to be given access to the truly vital information—the truly inside stuff—than the manager of millions, tens of millions, maybe billions of dollars of other people's money.

Money managers will protest this assertion, but it's a fact. It only makes sense.

It only makes sense that they attract all kinds of asset users. Venture capitalists seek them out. Securities analysts tantalize them with their juiciest numbers. Investment bankers present them with a parade of surefire deals. Plain stockbrokers pull out all the stops to please them. Well-placed private investors come up with good information too. And don't forget the investment advisers—bagmen. Without the money managers, they would die.

Here's a classic case of how it works. It's an old story in that these events began in 1967 but a new story because it has not been revealed until right now. Mainly, however, this is an instructive story of pure, classic, unadulterated insider trading.

In the late 1960s and early 1970s, the Shah of Iran was at the height of his power. He was one of this country's few unwavering supporters in the Middle East. We had Israel and the Shah on our side in this arena of the Cold War, and that was about it. In the spring of 1967 the Shah traveled to Washington, D.C., to confer with President Lyndon Johnson on matters of mutual interest. Of course, LBJ was at that time beleaguered by the war in Vietnam, but he could always make time for the Shah.

Traveling with the Shah was a close associate whom I shall refer to as "Hushang." This young man had studied at a European university, and it was there that he met an American I shall call "Carl Smith."

Carl's father had been with the U.S. military in the Middle East for many years. Carl was born and received his early schooling there, and thus he and Hushang had much in common when they met at the same university in Europe. They became fast friends. They maintained their friendship after Carl graduated and returned to New York City to work on Wall Street.

Carl's first job was as an associate analyst. Three years later he was recruited by another firm as a stockbroker. A quiet, diminutive man with an almost perfect ability to remember historical details, Carl took to the business and the business took to him. He moved up the corporate ladder to become one of the managing partners. It was in this position that he became the money manager for Hushang's $2 million personal portfolio, among many portfolios that large and much larger. Hushang almost always welcomed Carl's ideas on stock purchases; his holdings were performing nicely. Before the Shah's visit in 1967, however, Carl hadn't heard from Hushang in several years. Things were quiet. But he knew that Hushang was accompanying the Shah and was hoping to get in touch with him when the party stopped off at the Waldorf-Astoria in New York.

But he didn't have to reach Hushang. The Iranian called Carl, who was surprised and delighted by the voice on the other end of the line. "Hi, Carl," Hushang said. "I'm in New York with the Shah. We're going to Washington tomorrow to visit LBJ. How about dinner? Do you have anything planned this evening?"

The truth is, it would not have mattered even if Carl had had anything planned that evening. He would have canceled any occasion short of the birth of a child to see his old friend again. He immediately agreed to meet Hushang at La Cote Basque, one of Carl's favorite restaurants, at eight o'clock.

Hushang arrived promptly, and Carl noted that his old friend was still the Hollywood prototype for the dark, handsome Middle Eastern gentleman. Carl had always envied his friend's perfect set of gleaming white teeth and shock of thick black hair. For his own part, Carl still had all his teeth but the hairs were dwindling to a precious few, carefully arranged atop his otherwise gleaming pate.

Drinks were served—vodka and tonic—and Hushang got down to the business at hand. Carl wasn't surprised that Hushang had more on his mind than a social call. He had sensed over the phone that Hushang's voice seemed unusually high. Something was afoot. Now he was about to hear what it was.

"Remember that oil company I talked to you about two years ago?" Hushang began.

"Wasn't that 'Midwest Oil?'" Michael recalled. In fact, the Shah's family had the controlling interest in Midwest Oil, which had huge oil-producing properties in the Middle East and was listed on the New York Stock Exchange.

"Righto!" said Hushang with exactly the same smile as

his old friend the Shah. It was a charming smile, but it was accompanied by a dead-cold seriousness in the eyes. He continued in a whisper, "The company will be hot. Very hot. Buy a million shares for yourself, pal."

Hushang continued with some descriptions of his acquaintances who were managing the company, but all in all was vague about why exactly Carl should invest his own money in Midwest Oil. But Carl had complete trust in his old friend. The following day he placed huge orders for Midwest Oil—not a million shares but *plenty* of shares in case the stock took off. The price was right at $26. Now all Carl could do was sit and wait. Hushang had flown down to Washington with the Shah.

Carl did not have to wait long. Within three days Midwest Oil was in orbit, trading at $75. Two weeks later it was a shooting star at $100.

Carl had trusted his friend. He had expected profits from the tip, but he had not expected a small fortune. His personal account was about a million ahead in just a few days. He had always suspected that the Shah's visit with LBJ in Washington had had something to do with Hushang's tip, but now he knew that some choice inside information had been making the rounds on the Street before any official announcement. That was the only way to explain the 300 percent rise in Midwest Oil shares in less than a month.

As I said, this was a classic case of insider trading by a large number of participants. When the Securities and Exchange Commission is confronted with such a flagrant instance of suspicious trading, the usual response is to announce that the stock is "being investigated." As often as not, that's the last anyone hears of it. Occasionally a report is issued. Perhaps there are just too many cases for too few investigators. However, things may change to some extent because the new head of the SEC, Arthur Levitt, is a former president of the American Stock Exchange. He knows the secrets of the Street, and my understanding is that he's determined to do what he can to clean things up. We shall see.

What was this information making the rounds regarding Midwest Oil? As Hushang well knew long before he urged Carl to buy Midwest Oil, the Shah was flying to the United States specifically to forge an arms-for-oil deal with LBJ, and Hushang was confident that the Shah could pull it off. (In fact, this unprecedented deal was something of a precursor to the ill-fated arms-for-hostages/Iran-Contra scandal that embarrassed the Reagan/Bush administration in late 1986.)

The Shah desperately needed certain military aircraft and weapons systems. In return, he would pay the United States with oil, which this country desperately needed at the time (and at all other times, for that matter). The deal would assure that the United States could avert an oil shortage. It was a brilliant plan, a strategic coup for both the Shah and LBJ.

And Midwest Oil would be a tremendous winner too, because Iran would buy every drop it could produce, at top dollar. That was the information leaking out of Washington that propelled Midwest Oil from $26 to $100 practically overnight and made Carl Smith and friends each a swift million or so for their personal accounts.

However, and to Carl's regret, the story of the meteoric

ascent of Midwest Oil does not end on that high note. When Lyndon Johnson decided not to seek the renomination of the Democratic party in 1968 in order to devote his full energies to winning, or at least concluding, the war in Vietnam, Richard Nixon won the election and took up residence in the White House in January, 1969.

Just four months later, on May 19, to be exact, Carl Smith received another phone call from his old friend. A couple of years earlier his friend's voice had been high-pitched with excitement. This time it was again high, but with a difference. This time his friend was nervous, even distraught. Carl could sense the tension. There were no preliminaries.

"Midwest Oil. Remember Midwest Oil, Carl? Sell."

"Sell?"

"Yes. Sell everything you've still got. Sell mine too. All of it."

Stunned, Carl rang off, phoned his trader on the floor of the Big Board, and whispered, "Liquidate the goddamn Midwest Oil. Yes, Pete, all of it. *Midwest Oil.* But don't create a panic. Do it sweet and easy. But get rid of the sucker fast."

Carl sank back in his leather chair and covered his face with his hands, literally shaking like a leaf. He was still highly exposed in the stock. So was Hushang. So were other customers. If Pete wasn't able to beat the market with those orders....

Carl was fortunate. Thanks to this second tip from Hushang, he was able to reach the sidelines before Midwest Oil crashed to $50. He lost some of the gains he had made earlier on the stock, but on the whole Carl made out well with Midwest Oil.

And what was Hushang's inside information this time around? Simple. Nixon had not liked the Shah's arms-for-oil deal with LBJ and had scrapped it. Moments after the news of this decision had reached the Shah in Teheran and well before it began to circulate within the administration in Washington, Hushang was on the phone to Carl in New York with that second, equally vital tip.

Money managers like Carl Smith and Bob Cummings are just as important to their clients as a lawyer is to his or her clients. What's more, this relationship is more genial and, well, fun. This relationship is not based on stress. You don't call your money manager only when you're about to be sued or arrested. It's fairly rare that inside information provides foreknowledge of impending doom, as with Hushang's second tip to Carl. More often the insider's scoop is on the upside, like Hushang's first tip. Usually money managers—good ones, at least, and unlike lawyers—don't cost you money. They make you money. That is fun.

The money manager is a trusted adviser, perhaps even an estate executor, certainly a confidant. This trusting relationship gives the manager a lot of elbow room. He or she can "redesign" a given piece of information so that it benefits not only the client but also his or her personal account. In addition, the money manager is in full charge of discretionary accounts and can do whatever he or she wishes with the clients' money, especially over the short run. Finally, the requirement for confidentiality in all manager-client relationships becomes a cloak that can hide whatever magic and miracles the manager is pulling off.

In short, money managers constitute an exclusive club that operates, the SEC notwithstanding, with very little oversight. Given these circumstances, given human nature, and given the requirement to "perform" at or above the level of their peers, insider trading is almost a given with money managers.

The Midwest Oil caper was Carl Smith's first experience with insider trading. It was also a choice lesson in the truth of the old cliché "Easy come, easy go," which can apply on Wall Street as well as it does everywhere else. Still, that Middle Eastern roller coaster whetted Carl's appetite for the next big play. He had no qualms about trading on inside information. He was just determined to avoid being whipsawed again. And he never was. Today Carl Smith is retired, living in the proverbial lap of luxury in an enormous Manhattan apartment, trading stocks for his own account and for a few close friends, including his pal and members of the former Shah's extended family.

Tipping the Tipster

Sometimes Street insiders receive inside information. At other times they *make their own*—a terrific play and not as difficult to pull off as it might sound. And nobody in the business is better positioned than a money manager to manufacture scoops.

To see how this works, I'll introduce a woman whom I'll call "Carol Teves," a young, diligent, and scrupulous public relations executive in New York City. On this particular Wednesday morning she was working away at her desk when she received a call from a man I will call "Ken Jones," an acquaintance of long standing, although the two hadn't talked for about a year. Ken is about ten years older than Carol. The earth moved just a tiny bit for Carol when she heard Ken's voice. He was a good-looking guy whom she had dated a few times several years earlier, and he was also a portfolio manager for a well-known investment manager.

Or at least he had been with the financier the last time they had spoken. Carol didn't know what percentage of the financier's empire of mutual funds and asset management groups Ken had helped handle, but any percentage at all would still be a lot of money. She had been impressed by her friend's standing in the financial world.

After the usual catching up about her personal life, which revealed that Carol had indeed married the guy she had been dating a year earlier (but no kids yet), she asked in as casual a manner as she could manage whether Ken was still with his old firm.

"Oh, yeah. 'Capital Management Fund.' And my job is getting better. We're doing lots of stuff, hot stuff, you know."

Let's get right to the point, Ken thought. Mustering as casual a tone as he could, Ken asked, "Say, Carol, are you still handling Franklin Industries?"

"Sure am. They're one of my oldest and best clients."

"Franklin," as I will call this company, is a maker of apparel for mass-merchandise retailers such as Sears, K-Mart, Target, and Avon Products.

"Well, could you arrange for me to meet James Tender?"

"Tender"—a pseudonym—was the chairman and CEO of Franklin. Ken had seen a small notice in *The New York Times* to the effect that Tender was coming to town to address an industry luncheon.

Carol didn't hesitate. "Sure, that would be terrific."

She penciled in a meeting for Tuesday afternoon with Tender, subject to confirming it with the man himself. But she was certain that Tender would be happy to meet Ken because the Capital name goes a long way on Wall Street. And Carol and Ken agreed to get together for drinks the evening before in Sir Harry's lounge at the Waldorf. She was married now, but what could be the harm? This was business, not pleasure, and certainly did not constitute a rekindling of the old flame.

Actually, the evening turned out to be business *and* pleasure. Mixed in with the bottles of superb chardonnay and the queries about Franklin Industries, Ken managed a few mild and not so mild flirtations. Carol knew she would flirt with Ken and maybe give in just a bit, but she would not end up in bed with him. No way. But Ken was getting amorous. Is he fishing for an affair or for information on Franklin? Carol asked herself. Ken kissed her in the mouth, hard and persistently. She kissed back as eagerly. His hand slipped under Carol's short skirt, as if to signal that she should grab his hand, or for the rest of the evening forget about resisting. Oh, God, what am I doing? I'm having an affair right here in the lounge of the Waldorf-Astoria! Then she closed her eyes, took a deep breath.

The following morning Carol woke with a start. What had she told Ken Jones about Franklin Industries? Had she really told him about the new contract with the major pharmaceutical giant, "Medco," as I will refer to it, for a new product? She thought she might have, late in the evening, maybe right after the third bottle of wine had been presented for their tipsy pleasure. Was this insider information? Would Ken use it to take a plunge on Franklin? Would Medco find out about the leak and cancel the contract and her job along with it? But it wasn't that big a deal anyway, Carol tried to reassure herself. After all, Tender, in an interview a couple of weeks earlier with the Dow-Jones News Service, had even alluded to a new contract with a major pharmaceutical company. Carol had been surprised when she had read that, but the stock had stayed right where it was—at $7. So relax, she told herself.

But just to be safe Carol pulled Ken aside the following afternoon before he went in for his meeting with Tender. "Ken, I don't know what you want to ask Mr. Tender, but I guess I told you about the new contract with Medco."

"That'll lead to bigger things, won't it?" Ken replied.

"Ken, I don't think you should let Tender know that you know about the contract. If you do, he'll know you found out from me. Please, just try to fish it out of him on your own. Okay?"

"Sure."

In the meeting between the analyst and the CEO of Franklin, Ken started off with the following boilerplate question: "Let's get started by talking about your products and whatever new ones you have in the pipeline and how they would impact sales next quarter and next year. Should I expect that you'll exceed the Street's bottom-line expectations?"

The tanned and silver-haired Tender replied with the boilerplate answer he gave to any and all analysts. In fact, it was the standard road show presentation Carol had helped him prepare, and it was an excellent one in his opinion. When

Tender was finished, Ken declared that he too was pleased with the show and then declared that he needed some more specifics in order to make his final determination.

"One of the companies that may want to enter your market is Medco, am I right?"

Carol gulped. She had asked Ken to maneuver Tender into being the first to mention Medco. But then Ken continued: "I hear it might even be interested in a merger with Franklin, mainly because of one of the products you've developed."

Carol relaxed. That was clever. That business about a merger would deflect Tender from wondering where Ken's information about Medco might have come from. And Tender answered enthusiastically: "Yes, indeed, Ken. Medco may want to play on our block, at least in some of our markets." Tender went on to explain in the tried and true language (if not the results) of synergy how the giant Medco could make strategic use of the relatively tiny Franklin's market. Then Tender added, "And it's also true, Ken, that Medco is very interested in one of our products. Uh, you know, Ken, Medco might yet become one of our bigger clients, if not the biggest, one day."

"That sounds great," Ken said. "And what's that product?"

His voice was innocence itself.

Tender hesitated just a moment. Then he said, "I'm going to tell you."

Carol was on the edge of her seat. She didn't know whether to feel relieved or concerned. Certainly she was going to be off the hook, but was it really in Franklin's best interest to make the information public at that time? Carol had been informed pointedly that Medco didn't want a big deal made out of this contract for this new product, a panty for the "older market" lined with absorbent cotton and with extra plastic to prevent leaking.

Tender described the product to Ken and then acknowledged that his company had signed a contract with Medco to deliver $1 million worth of this underwear. "We are confident that there's a huge market for these, but nothing guarantees that. But with Medco in the act, the product could become a really big seller," Tender said with a smile that implied to Ken and to Carol that a lot more was going on in this regard than he could reveal at the time.

Soon the three participants called the meeting a wrap, each with a good reason to be pleased with the results. Ken was certainly sold on the new Franklin product. He told his trader that afternoon to begin loading up on Franklin at the opening bell the following morning. "Just keep me posted on what's going on," Ken said. For the next three days he followed the stock like a hawk.

Meanwhile, Carol was nervous. Ken hadn't told her in so many words, but she thought he was moving Capital's money and some of his own into Franklin, and she knew that this trading was based on information that went way beyond what had been publicly announced. After a couple of days she called her friend and said, "Ken, I don't want to get in trouble with the SEC, and I'm sure you don't either."

"I didn't want to tell you this," Ken replied, "but yes, I've been buying a bucketful of shares. I think it's a super winner, Carol. I have to buy." He ignored Carol's reference to the SEC and insider trading, trying to banish the subject from her mind.

Then Ken added, "But what's the deal, Carol? Why hasn't a word been said about the product and Medco? Aren't you going to issue a press release?"

Frustrated, Carol replied, "Ken, I *told* you, Medco doesn't want to make a big deal out of this. We mentioned a new contract in the press conference, and that's as much as we want to disclose."

"Okay, fine, but I think you people are making a big mistake. You *should* go ahead and make a big deal out of this, for God's sake, because it's a damned big thing with potentially big results for Franklin and for Medco."

Carol and Ken rang off. Two days later Franklin stock spiked $3 to $10. It was one of the biggest percentage gainers on the American exchange. Carol had been watching the tape closely. She was on the phone before Ken could leave his office for the day.

"What's going on, Ken? Why has Franklin gone crazy? Tender's concerned because he doesn't know why the stock is so active."

"Jesus, Carol. The stock should go up! It's a good company, and it's good stock with rich potential. You've said so yourself. I feel very good about it. Thank you."

That was very nice but beside the point for Carol. She repeated her question: "Ken, tell me what you really think is going on."

"Well, to tell you the truth, I heard that Dan Dorfman went on the tube today with this thing about Franklin's new panties and Medco's new contract. You know, that story."

Of course, Ken had not just "heard" that Dorfman had been on the air with the story, but he had good reason to waffle with Carol. He realized that this information was going to infuriate his friend, and he was correct.

"Ken, did you tell Dorfman?" Carol asked.

"Me?! Dorfman has tons of sources."

That was true enough.

After hanging up with Ken, Carol was tempted to call Dorfman himself regarding the leak. But why bother? He wouldn't waste his time justifying to some PR flak why he had reported on a company. Let it drop, Carol decided.

By coincidence, several weeks later Carol and Franklin's CEO, James Tender, found themselves dining in the same restaurant as Dan Dorfman and a companion. When Carol pointed out the columnist-broadcaster to Tender, the CEO immediately said he would ask Dorfman about the Medco leak. Franklin stock had continued to climb in the two weeks since Dorfman's statement—it eventually reached $14, after starting the run at $7. Tender was happy about that vote of confidence from the markets, but he had also revealed to Carol earlier that Medco had been more than serious about not wanting to make a big deal about the contract. The giant company had informed Franklin that now it might never get another dollar out of what might have been its biggest customer. Medco apparently wanted to keep the information secret until it made the announcement itself. In the long run, Tender knew, the inside tip could only hurt Franklin. Tender was determined to find out where it had come from. He brushed aside Carol's suggestion that perhaps he should just let the matter go.

Looming over Dan Dorfman's table, Tender introduced himself as the CEO of Franklin Industries and then said, "You remember, you mentioned our stock on television."

"Of course I remember. The stock had a nice run, too."

"Tell me, sir, I'm dying to know. Was it Ken Jones of Capital Management who gave you that tip on us?"

"Absolutely," Dorfman replied with a big smile. It's unusual for a journalist to identify a source, but in this case Dorfman apparently felt that Tender knew Ken Jones well enough and didn't feel obligated to shield the source of the story.

Tender nodded his head and returned to his table.

By early 1994, a little over a year after this occurred, Franklin stock had retreated all the way back to the starting point and then some. A major reason was that the big contract with Medco had failed to materialize. But was Ken Jones shedding any tears for Franklin? Hardly. His job was to worry about the short run for the Capital portfolio and for his own. Franklin's long-term problems were not his concern then or ever. He had made out quite well from the $1 million contract with Medco that never panned out. It was a job well done for Ken.

Carol Teves feels uneasy to this day about the whole Franklin episode, although she has not lost the account. She has not heard from Ken Jones since.

The Gate-*Crashers*

There are money managers. And then there are *money managers*. The one I'm about to describe is a different kind of money manager entirely. He plays in a league different from that of Ken Jones, Bob Cummings, and Carl Smith. His name? Like many of the characters in this book, I can't reveal his identity. But he's alive and well and thriving on the Street. So for now, I'll have to call him "Max Rosenthal." Rosenthal was a young analyst in the 1960s when he decided that he wanted to be his own boss. The rest, as they say, is history. Now Max is one of the most famous and notorious, as well as one of the wealthiest, hedge fund managers in the business. While Carl Smith might be considered something of a middleweight on the Street, Max Rosenthal is an ultraheavyweight with an enormous ego and an obsession to win. You do not trifle with this particular Max.

No guts, no glory? Max forever seeks glory, and he has the guts to deliver on his ambition.

While Carl Smith deals in millions and tens of millions of dollars, Max Rosenthal plays catch with tens and *hundreds* of millions. Rosenthal and his peers are not mere gatekeepers. They wield so much power on the Street, I think of them more as gate-*crashers*. And they're fearless by definition. As the dynamo behind his New York–based firm, Rosenthal is not afraid to put a good percentage of his fund's many billions in assets behind some of the longest shots on Wall Street.

Or are they long shots after all? Maybe not. It all depends on the quality of the information. Still, high risk goes with the territory in hedge funds, which are in essence private funds that use the megaassets of only the wealthiest investors. By keeping the number of investors below 100, the hedge fund avoids almost all the reporting regulations which at least try to hem in the money managers of corporate pension funds and mutual funds. (However, this genial state of affairs for the hedge funds may change. They have never been particularly popular on staid Wall Street, where they're seen as highly speculative and as a vehicle for short sellers. They are also suspected of harboring "hot money" emanating from overseas sources, for the most part, that are seeking those highly speculative plays and the correspondingly high returns. Thus, the hedge funds are blamed for adding to the market's volatility. But now the powers that be in Washington, led by the House Banking Committee, are expected to take a hard look at the tremendous and unregulated clout of the hedges.)

Any hedge fund has a minimum investment, sometimes $1 million, sometimes as high as $5 million (Rosenthal's minimum happens to be $1 million). Of course, there's no maximum. It's understood by the investor that the hedge fund manager will not be deterred by the risks of near infinity that go with the territory in futures, derivatives, short selling, options, overseas action, and the other plays that are the bread and butter of hedge funds. Such risks are necessary in order to achieve the extraordinarily high returns these funds posted with near regularity during the bull market of the late 1980s and early 1990s.

As a fee, the fund manager pockets a percentage of the profits, often 20 percent, but in the case of losses, the investor is on his or her own. (Of course, this is also true with mutual funds or an individual money manager.) The hedge fund operator will provide a résumé—past results—but this is hardly a guarantee. Informally, some operators will direct you to satisfied clients. This is fine, but it should be understood that they will not direct you to any unsatisfied clients. If your hard-earned millions are burning a hole in your pocket and you're thinking about joining a hedge fund, and if you're also wondering what this action might cost you on the downside, keep in mind the old maxim "If you have to ask, you can't afford it."

In the short run, hedge funds can make you a billionaire or cost you everything. The daredevil investing of Max Rosenthal's firm yielded a hefty return in 1993, but the same style of gunslinging lost all that profit and then some in the first part of 1994. In that period Rosenthal lost a stunning sum of money, and it wasn't the first time he had taken a bath in red ink. His losses in the crash of October 1987 reached the $1 billion mark. To stem the hemorrhaging, he spent much of the rest of 1994 selling most of his holdings, including stocks and bonds, commodities, currencies, and derivatives. And this when the market was on the decline. Still, this was the Rosenthal way of doing things: big dramatic actions, even when it comes to dumping his holdings. Late in the year he had regrouped and was sitting on about $2 billion in cash. He denied to the financial press the persistent rumors that he's closing up shop, but there's no law against taking a year off.

How far will Max Rosenthal go in order to chalk up a giant score? Well, one former partner uses the polite term "edge" to describe what Max Rosenthal is always seeking before he takes a plunge.

What kind of edge exactly? Does Rosenthal engage in trading in inside information? Another former partner suggests that Max does not leave home without it. This investor, who contributed a lot of money to Rosenthal plays, told me, "Max thrives on the use of exclusively 'insidy,' if risky, tools. So he surrounds himself with people who can provide such treasures."

Inside information that's still risky information? How does this work? It sounds almost like a contradiction. Isn't the idea behind the best inside information to give the money manager a lock on the action? Theoretically, yes, but the juiciest information can also be the riskiest information. For one thing, you can go to prison. Remember Ivan Boesky? As I have discussed, he dealt with the best inside information anywhere—*perfect* information—but he went to jail for it.

It's one thing to be caught making $10,000 illegally. It's another thing entirely to be nailed making $100 million. The Feds don't like that.

What's more, perfect information may be perfect only for a very short period of time. In the case of inside information regarding a takeover, timing is of the essence. Positions can change overnight. They can change within minutes. The timing has to be perfect, as well as the information itself. The rewards can be enormous when one is trading "inside," but there are major risks too. Even giants such as Max Rosenthal can come up short in a battle of the inside information.

By way of illustration, let's return to a point in the 1980s, one of those high-flying years on Wall Street if there ever was one. In the summer of that year, one of Max's trusted partners whispered in his ear that he should "build a mountain of a stock position" in a major transportation company. (I'll call it "Transporco.")

"Why?" It was a fair question.

Because Transporco was about to be the target of a takeover plot by a supposedly cash-laden group of investors.

The moment Max Rosenthal received this tip, he did two things. He ordered his lieutenants to switch all their attention to this Transporco takeover plot. He wanted to know who the players were, and he wanted to know the numbers they were playing with. Almost simultaneously, he also ordered his chief trader to accumulate Transporco *muy rapido*, as Bob Cummings's secretary, Vivian, would put it. At the time the stock was trading in the $40 vicinity.

Within moments, it seemed, Rosenthal had amassed a 5 percent stake in the company. Nor did the lightning speed

with which Max positioned his fund vis-à-vis Transporco
surprise his lieutenants or the aficionados of the Street.
That's Max's style, to jump into a situation in a big way at
the merest hint of blood in the water. In fact, that propensity is almost an incurable affliction among hedge fund
managers. Michael Steinhardt and George Soros are two big
ones who come to mind, plunking down enormous sums of
money after making snap decisions, sometimes smart ones,
sometimes not so smart. Steinhardt, Soros, and their hedge
fund investors suffered huge losses in 1994.

In defense of hedge fund managers, quick decisions are
crucial in their business. You don't post the kind of numbers
Steinhardt Partners or George Soros are proud of by dillydal-
lying. You can't sit around waiting for Dan Dorfman to confirm the scoop on his midday CNBC broadcast. Dorfman's
information is usually solid, but is it always absolutely *fresh*?
That's the key. In the case of a takeover bid, any statement by
Dorfman or by anyone else would probably be too late. To borrow a crude phrase from *Bonfire of the Vanities*, "the big
swinging dicks" on the Street would already have made their
move.

In the case of Transporco, Rosenthal was certain he had
the inside track, and he was right. Sort of, as we'll see.

Soon enough, Rosenthal learned that an investor I will
call "David Morgenstein" was now operating on his own as
a raider and money runner, and was spearheading the takeover campaign. Max was informed that Morgenstein knew
about Max's big move in Transporco and would welcome
him as an ally in the raid. A meeting was set up.
Morgenstein came to the Rosenthal offices and acknowl-

edged his plan to go after the company in a buyout bid. Morgenstein knew that the company was on the brink of filing for Chapter 11.

Rosenthal continued buying Transporco stock, and the stock continued its upward ascent, from $40 to $52. When his stake approached nearly 10 percent, Rosenthal officially informed the chairman and CEO of the holding company. In a letter he also made an ominous threat, implying that if the company did not take urgent steps to salvage the company and lift it out of its financial hole, the Rosenthal gang might just be forced to engineer a takeover. They would align themselves with another group of shareholders to do the job. It was imperative that management understand the urgency of the problem and the very real possibility of losing control of the company. The shareholders were quickly losing patience.

Sincerely yours, Max Rosenthal.

Two things happened, one of which Rosenthal could and perhaps should have expected, the other of which was truly a low blow.

Predictably enough, those in Transporco management swung into action to save their jobs. One year after Rosenthal started buying shares in their stock, they protected their flank by selling a 12 percent stake in the company to a major outside—and friendly—investor. This was a friendly transaction, and with the passive investor now sitting on such a big stake, a hostile takeover of Transporco would have been almost impossible to pull off.

Max Rosenthal had paid an average of $39.50 for his nearly 10 percent stake. The day after the sale to the outside

investor the stock closed at $15. According to one of the for-
mer partners introduced earlier—an investor who lost about
$1 million in the caper that the outside investor shot
down—this particular mistake cost Rosenthal about $110
million, including all incidental expenses.

Adding insult to substantial injury, Rosenthal knew by
that time that the man he had thought was in his camp,
Morgenstein, had actually tossed him loaded dice. Before
the coup de grâce (the sale), while Transporco stock was still
climbing on the strength of the takeover possibility by the
Rosenthal group, Morgenstein had *sold* 2 million shares. He
was taking his gains and getting out.

Had Morgenstein *ever* intended to launch a takeover bid?
Had the initial tip to Rosenthal and the initial meeting
between the two men been an elaborate setup? If so, give
Morgenstein some credit. He pulled it off, and not many
men have had the nerve to play Max Rosenthal for a patsy.

The moral of this story: Trading on inside information
isn't without risk. At the highest levels, in fact, inside information is positively dangerous if it's not *perfect* and if the
timing's not perfect too.

One of Rosenthal's fellow hedge fund managers famil-
iar with the Transporco debacle blames it on the boss's
huge ego. "He's a stock jock who finds it hard to concede
he has made a mistake," this trader said. Rosenthal himself conceded to a friend that his ego had gotten in the
way of sound judgment in the failed play on Transporco. It

was no surprise, really. He told *Business Week* that one reason he was attracted to the hedge funds was that he was "cocky."

And then there's this telltale story from the mid-1980s, which gives us more insight into the ways of the most inconspicuous kind of inside trading—so inconspicuous, in fact, that it may be perfectly legal!

One June morning a Rosenthal associate whom I will call "Jerry" burst into the boss's office to ask permission to buy a large block of "Pharmco Group" stock.

"Why?"

Again, it was a good question. If an idea isn't his own, Max wants a great pitch based on solid inside information. If he hears it, he'll listen, and this was certainly the case in his dealings with Jerry, who was just as aggressive, confident, and egotistical as his boss.

Jerry continued: "The deal is I just saw Pharmco's chairman yesterday, and we had a pleasant chat. Very intimate chat. He showed me how well things have been going."

At the mention of a "very intimate chat" with the CEO of Pharmco, Max's interest flickered to life. "What's the stock doing?" he asked. The stock was trading at $42. One question Rosenthal did not ask was, Is this legal? He didn't *want* to know what Jerry had learned, and Jerry didn't want to tell him.

"We should take in 600,000, maybe 700,000 shares," Jerry urged. "Trust me, Max. I know the stock will spike from here."

Max was very tempted to trust Jerry, who had been a top analyst at a number of major Street firms. Jerry was a hustler from the Bronx—street-smart. He was probably right. Max played with some numbers on his computer terminal for a few minutes.

"C'mon, Max," Jerry pressed. "This will be a monster of a stock. We'll make tons here."

Finally Max relented. Within the hour Rosenthal bought 2 million shares at 39½. Not the 600,000 or 700,000 Jerry had recommended, but 2 million. Jerry was ecstatic when he saw the numbers flicker across the tape. Vintage Rosenthal. Vintage hedge fund manager. Take a huge position and hang on for the hairy ride.

The next day Max and Jerry got their spike, all the way to $47. Rosenthal cashed in 1.3 million shares, holding the 700,000 Jerry had wanted to buy in the first place. Net profit for the day's work: a cool $8 million. Not bad at all, even for Rosenthal.

Flush with the thrill of victory, Jerry wanted to congratulate Max for having confidence in him and for his gutsy, profit-packed plunge with the 2 million shares. But Max would have none of it. Already preoccupied with another deal, he glanced up from his desk and growled, "What do you want, Jerry? I'm busy."

"Yeah, so am I!" Jerry exploded, and charged for the door. One month later he quit Rosenthal's firm and founded his own small investment banking group, specializing in raising capital for small- to mid-size companies.

Two Spy Stories

Y ou just never know about tips on Wall Street. They come in all shapes and sizes and at the most unexpected moments. But one thing is for certain: The alert investor is ready to pounce when the ball takes a lucky bounce in his or her direction. One of the oddest "tips" I ever heard about and one that came at one of the most opportune moments involves none other than Boyd Jefferies, who previously ran his own trading firm, Jefferies & Company.

Jefferies has since been convicted of securities fraud. Specifically, he was one of Ivan Boesky's more efficient parking attendants. "Parking" stocks means hiding big blocks of shares to disguise their ownership. Boesky paid certain trader friends to hold the shares for him. By parking stock with co-conspirators, he was able to hide the real supply-and-demand situation in the stock. But then Boyd

Jefferies squealed on Boesky and confessed his own role in the scheme. Turning stoolie enabled Jefferies to escape an unwanted holiday behind bars. He was one of many who got away with the proverbial slap on the wrist—a two-month commuted prison sentence plus a modest fine of $200,000.

Earlier in the red-hot 1980s, however, Jefferies had been right up there with Mike Steinhardt as a money pro and master trader in the middle of the LBO action. With the phrase "money pro" I draw a distinction between Jefferies and the traditional money manager. Although he does indeed invest money for clients, Jefferies's brand of trading is much more speculative than that of the standard money manager. His kind of work requires speed, timing, and bravado. In terms of spicy, if risky, bets on stocks, he's an octave above most of the other money managers who figure in this book.

Jefferies & Company was and is based in Los Angeles, but the man himself operated out of the fourth floor of a handsome Iranian-owned building at 54th Street and Fifth Avenue in Manhattan, the building that used to house the Piaget headquarters. There were no nameplates on the doors on that fourth floor. (Not coincidentally, perhaps, the top floor of the same building was one of Ivan Boesky's glorious domiciles. These offices had previously been occupied by Marc Rich, a notorious securities, commodities, and currency trader who fled the United States in 1983 to avoid tax evasion charges.)

One morning in September 1986 the same news item caught the eye of all the Jefferies traders reading their morning supply of newspapers. According to *The Wall Street Journal*, Canadian financier Robert Campeau, one of the real takeover terrors of the time, had made a hostile move against Allied Stores, the department store chain, at $70 a share. Boyd Jefferies and friends placed this tidbit of information in their quiver and followed events at a distance. Soon enough, real estate mogul Tony DeBartolo showed up at the takeover table with a larger offer of $77 a share. Now Boyd decided that it was time to reserve a seat at that table.

"Sweep the street," he directed his chief trader, Steve Mindnich. A "sweep" is a buying blitz to corner and effectively control the stock of a particular company. It is now also illegal, having been banned by the SEC in 1990. When sweeping was legal, not every brokerage house could pull it off—very few could—but this kind of action had been one of Jefferies's specialties since the house was founded in 1962. The company also brings together institutional buyers and institutional sellers, executing trades over the counter and outside the purview of the stock exchanges. This way, there's less of a chance that the price will run away from the level at which both buyer and seller want it. The fees for this kind of service are enormous.

Tony DeBartolo and Robert Campeau would also have wanted to sweep the Street for Allied shares, but to do so they would have had to rely on their investment bankers. Boyd Jefferies didn't have to rely on anyone but his own shop.

Steve Mindnich was on the phone before his coffee was cold, armed with a list of Allied's major shareholders.

Was Jefferies & Company prepared to pay a premium for shares of Allied Stores? The fast-talking Mindnich assured the prospective sellers that the company was indeed willing to pay a premium. At the time the stock was selling at $60, and DeBartolo's bid had been for $77. Stacks of shares began accumulating in the Jefferies portfolio, costing between $78 and $82. In just a few days Mindnich and his raider-traders acquired 44 million shares of the company—51 percent.

This was a remarkable performance. Sometimes sweeping was not possible at all. It was easier when the shares were concentrated in the hands of a few investors and institutions, but it was never easy. Sometimes the shareholders wanted to play hardball too. When they sensed a takeover battle, they waited for the highest bidder. Nothing said they had to sell to Mindnich. But enough of them did.

What was going on here? Why did this relatively small trading shop suddenly own the controlling interest in the target of a takeover play? Boyd Jefferies thought that this battle between DeBartolo and Campeau was for real, that they would fight to the death, and that they would get into a bidding war, if necessary, for the Jefferies stake. Of course, Jefferies had no interest whatsoever in acquiring Allied for himself and his company. He was a stock trader, not a corporate raider, and he didn't want to be a department store executive. But his controlling share in the stock now gave him not only a seat at the table but the ace in the hole, the swing card itself. He could demand his price when the battle began.

Which of the raiders would pay the most for this swing card? That was the question. Mindnich and most of the other leading strategists at Jefferies thought that DeBartolo would pay, but Boyd Jefferies and one or two others surmised that Campeau had the determination and wherewithal to win. In any event, there was nothing to do but find out. Shares in hand, Mindnich called DeBartolo directly and told him he could help DeBartolo win Allied. All the shares were DeBartolo's at $84 each.

DeBartolo was less than responsive. He considered that price too steep. He wasn't even sure Jefferies & Company was being straight with him. Did they actually own all the stock they claimed to own? These young, preppie-looking guys from Wall Street were trying to muscle in on Tony DeBartolo? The real estate magnate didn't like it. He wanted time to mull over his options.

Time, Mindnich replied, is one thing you don't own. This Allied stock is another. Our final offer is $84, take it or leave it.

This was a dangerous game Boyd and Mindnich were playing. This was not really their jigger of Jack Daniels. They didn't want 51 percent of Allied Stores, not for any longer than was absolutely necessary.

Meanwhile, that same afternoon, a Jefferies spy relayed the news to Jefferies and Mindnich that Robert Campeau had been seen lurking around the board of directors room at the First Boston offices on 52d Street. This was the tip I mentioned at the beginning of the story. This was the innocent-looking (and perfectly legal) information that allowed all the pieces to fall into place for Boyd Jefferies.

Boyd had known that First Boston was the investment bank hired by Campeau to nail down the Allied Stores takeover. Obviously, Campeau was now in the First Boston offices discussing strategy with his advisers. Obviously, Campeau wanted Allied Stores. *Obviously*, Campeau was more willing than DeBartolo was to buy out Jefferies.

Mindnich and the senior managing director, Lou Bellucci, raced over to First Boston to offer Campeau what DeBartolo had just turned down: 51 percent of the shares. Like DeBartolo, Campeau was initially shocked and suspicious about the offer. Forget grabbing for the brass ring. These Jefferies traders were offering him Allied Stores on a silver platter. Go ahead and give 'em a seat at the table, but were they playing with a full deck?

Campeau retired to huddle with the First Boston people. Then he called in Bellucci and Mindnich. They talked. Campeau also wanted more time, and he wanted the Jefferies group to come down to a "more reasonable price level." Failing that, he wanted to negotiate easier terms for the payment, something of a payment plan. Mindnich and Bellucci relented somewhat on a timetable of staggered payments, but they dug in on the question of price, making it clear that this huge block of shares was in danger of going to someone else if the people in that room couldn't agree on a price.

After five minutes Campeau announced, "Yes, I want all those shares!"

The deal was consummated at $84 a share. The math on the Allied Stores caper is easy. At a profit between $2 and $6 a share for 44 million shares, Boyd Jefferies and his team scooped off the table a gross profit of somewhere between a measly $88 million and a respectable $264 million—minus, I assume, crosstown taxi fares and the sizable gratuity bestowed on the spy who saw Robert Campeau hanging around the First Boston offices.

Not only do tips come in all shapes and sizes and at the most unexpected moments, sometimes they backfire. Sometimes the ball takes a very bad bounce. Nor is it surprising that the following story illustrating that point involves the California-based Feshbach brothers, who were famous in the 1980s for looking at the dark side of any corporation. They specialized in short-selling techniques. If a corporate executive heard that these brothers, Kurt, Matt, and Joe, had taken an interest in his or her company, that could only be bad news for the company but often good news for the Feshbachs, because they did quite well taking the short route to the bank. At one point they had amassed assets of more than $1 billion. Mike Steinhardt, George Soros, and any number of heavyweight hedge fund operators were not ashamed to honor the Feshbachs by aping their strategies.

For years it seemed as if the Feshbachs could do no wrong in their selection of weak stocks. Then one day they got burned badly, and one of the culprits might have been information that backfired. Another culprit is short sell-ing. It is inherently dangerous. *Caveat venditor.*

The company in question is LyphoMed, Inc., a small biotech firm that produces and sells multivitamins as well as antibiotic, anticancer, cardiovascular, anesthesia, and steroid products. The company went public in May 1983 and imme-diately proved to be a hot offering, in large part because a major Japanese pharmaceutical company began to load up on its stock. Fujisawa eventually acquired 30 percent of the 30 million shares outstanding. This kind of endorsement and support "within the industry" often provides a solid foundation for just about any stock.

Four years later, in the summer of 1987, a few months before the market crash, LyphoMed was trading in the low $30s. That was the good news for company management. The bad news was that the Feshbachs had their eye on the stock, whether management knew it or not. The Feshbachs started shorting the stock heavily. Shortly thereafter sever-al negative articles about LyphoMed hit the financial press. What a strange coincidence, noted one trader of my acquaintance. Of course, this trader was perfectly happy to see the articles because he had done a little shorting of LyphoMed for himself.

Rumors about LyphoMed multiplied. One of the most serious was a report that the company was under investiga-tion by the Food and Drug Administration (FDA). That kind of rumor, if subsequently confirmed, can be the death knell for a small company in that field. And the report did prove to be true, because FDA inspectors moved into LyphoMed's facility at Melrose Park, Illinois, in July.

How did the shorts know that the FDA was about to pull a raid on LyphoMed? The agency itself was curious, but an in-house investigation proved fruitless. In any event, investors didn't care about the source of the leak. The stock skidded to the high teens. Then the official report of the investigators was issued in October, just before the market crash. The FDA found that the company had failed to comply with certain mandated manufacturing standards.

This report plus Black Monday knocked LyphoMed all the way down to $10, where it lingered for a while before beginning a rebound which brought it back to $22 in December. Even if they hadn't covered their short positions when the stock had plunged to $10, the Feshbachs and other short sellers were still nicely positioned to cash in. Some did so, but others, including the Feshbachs, wanted even more profit. They were looking at the impact of the FDA affair over the long haul. Would it unduly delay the introduction of new drugs? Very possibly. Therefore, the Feshbachs passed up the opportunity to take what remained of a paper profit that had been more than $50 million at one point. One of the shorts who cashed out said that the brothers were convinced that the company would go bust.

By contrast, the LyphoMed bulls thought that the company had simply grown too fast and had not paid enough attention to quality-control measures. Maybe there weren't many of these intrepid souls, but in August 1988, less than a year after the negative FDA report, the bulls got their reward when it turned out that Fujisawa Pharmaceuticals was leading the herd. The Japanese firm took advantage of the stock's battered price and tendered for the LyphoMed shares it didn't already own at $31 a share.

The offer was gladly accepted, of course. But why did the Japanese firm offer such a premium? Presumably because it did not want to lose face by offering a price lower than what it had already paid for its 30 percent stake in the company.

What a hit for the shorts! From a paper profit of more than $50 million, they lost about that much on LyphoMed. The Feshbachs had been correct about the FDA raid, and their timing against the other negative reports was perfect but in betting that LyphoMed would go bust, they failed to pay attention to the company's intrinsic value.

The FDA raid might have been tipped by insiders, and it would definitely have paid short-term dividends. But the *perfect* inside information would have revealed the Fujisawa move, and this information the Feshbachs did not have. As it turned out, there must have been a lot of information the Feshbachs did not have. In the face of the belligerent bull market that followed the 1987 crash, the short-selling Feshbachs lost a lot of their mystique and about nine-tenths of their assets as well. By the end of 1993 that number was down from $1 billion-plus to $100 million.

Infighting Among the Insiders

Carl Icahn is not a money manager. By no stretch of the imagination is he a "mere" money manager. Nevertheless, this seems like the appropriate time and place to relate a short story about this famous raider. After all, the other incidents in the preceding chapters have dealt with market machinations at the highest levels. This story fits right into that context.

There is no honor among thieves. This is a fact. What about honor among takeover specialists and other Wall Street titans? That happens ... occasionally, I would say. Alas, this brief story about Carl Icahn was not one of those occasions.

Icahn was and still is one of the more controversial names on the Street, known initially as one of the most feared takeover artists and then as the chairman and CEO of Trans World Airlines (TWA). Owning an airline had been a dream since Icahn's early days as a broker for Dreyfus. Owning an airline would cap his career as a takeover titan. Owning an airline would put him in the same league as the legendary Howard Hughes.

And as it turned out, owning an airline would bankrupt that airline.

With all the problems TWA encountered after Icahn took over in the late 1980s, we tend to forget that it was a moneymaking enterprise at the time. Now Icahn is out, and the airline is owned by three unions, nonunion employees, and its creditors (who have the lion's share of 55 percent). It emerged from Chapter 11 after a restructuring in November 1993, but the nation's seventh largest airline may yet have to file for protection a second time. Either that or issue more common and preferred shares—300 million would be a nice, round number and one guaranteed to dilute everyone's current shareholdings. But something has to be done, because there's the problem of all that debt left over from the Icahn takeover.

About $1.8 billion worth. Most of it due fairly soon: $225 million in 15 percent secured notes in 1998, $332 million in 8 percent secured notes in 2000, and $129 million in 8¾ percent secured aircraft financing notes, payable through the end of the decade.

Then there's the final $190 million of a $200 million secured loan held by—who else?—the former CEO. The debt situation is so onerous that TWA's management and the investment bankers have come up with a plan to issue common shares to pay some of the creditors for some of the TWA paper they are currently holding.

This restructuring might help the airline, or TWA might never recover from the experience of being owned by Carl Icahn. Either way, the raider himself has emerged a winner financially, which is the way it usually goes in these circles. It's certainly the way it usually goes with this particular investing giant, who has been resourceful, cunning, and ruthless since his days on the boxing team at Princeton and since those earliest days at Dreyfus, when he was among just 15 brokers hired from a group of 500 applicants and worked for $100 week as a trainee.

Another one of the Dreyfus brokers hired that day was Bob Berlin, whom we will soon meet in another chapter. Icahn and Bob Berlin remain good friends. Berlin has seen his buddy bluff and bluster his way to victory in many situations and would not be surprised about how Icahn put one over on fellow raider and onetime friend Bennet LeBow.

Our story starts with Ben LeBow owning the controlling interest in New Valley Corp., which is the parent of Western Union. In the summer of 1989 LeBow invited Icahn and his wife and another raider type, Leon Black (formerly a Mike Milken crony at the now defunct Drexel Burnham Lambert), and his wife to join the LeBows on their yacht in the Mediterranean. Everyone had a swell time. Ben LeBow now considered Carl Icahn a friend.

By Christmas he considered him an enemy. Unbeknownst to LeBow, Icahn had been buying all available bonds issued by New Valley! When LeBow got wind of the purchases, Icahn already had 19 percent of the bonds. Eventually he collected 50 percent. So much for friendship, but LeBow had forgotten the old maxim that there are no friends in business, just temporary partners.

What was Icahn trying to pull with those bond purchases? He was convinced that New Valley was bankruptcy-bound and wanted to be a major debt holder. Any reorganization after bankruptcy would lead to the selling of assets and the paying off of creditors, including bondholders. And since Icahn was buying the bonds for about 30 cents on the dollar and would be paid off at least a dollar on the dollar, bankruptcy for his yachting companion's company would earn him a windfall profit, an insider's sweetest dream.

Now, why were these bonds available on the market at 30 cents in the first place? Enter Mike Milken. Most of Icahn's bonds were some of the $500 million worth sold by Milken for Western Union (now New Valley) in 1987. They were junk bonds. Other debt was also piling up for the company. It was on the brink of collapse. This was also right at the height of the junk bond scandal on Wall Street, and the holders of those bonds wanted out. Icahn was more than happy to relieve them of their burden.

It was a typical Icahn action. No one who knew him was surprised at his appetite for those junk bonds (he pulled a similar caper with the junk that financed Donald Trump's casinos). No one who knew Icahn was surprised that Ben LeBow, the man who had hosted him on a yacht cruise in the summer, would be cursing him by the time the snow was falling in the winter.

This time I do *not* exaggerate. LeBow does curse Icahn. He hisses with anger when the name comes up.

After acquiring the largest share of New Valley bonds, Icahn represented the bondholders at several meetings of the board of directors. At each of those meetings he agreed with the reorganization committee's recommended route to bankruptcy. But then he raised questions. A dozen meetings, a hundred questions. Sometimes LeBow walked out in anger, sometimes Icahn. LeBow was particularly incensed at Icahn's refusal to sell his bondholdings back to the company. "Why don't you sell like everybody else?" asked a frustrated LeBow. Icahn retorted: "Because you want them!"

But finally there was an agreement.

Finally, in March 1993, Chapter 11.

Finally, in September 1994, a court-supervised auction of assets, with the venerable 144-year-old Western Union going to First Financial Management of Atlanta for $1.19 billion.

Finally Ben LeBow is rid of Carl Icahn.

Or is he?! The final irony in this little story of infighting among the insiders is that a third raider type, Mark Dickstein, has entered the picture. While the proposed reorganization of New Valley will leave Ben LeBow in charge once the company emerges from bankruptcy, a group of shareholders has filed suit to kick LeBow out and replace him with Dickstein. This thirty-five-year-old investor has a reputation for extreme savvy in takeover and bankruptcy situations and for employing guerrilla tactics not unlike those favored by LeBow and Icahn. The upstart has been accumulating his own stake in New Valley's preferred shares.

But Icahn doesn't want Dickstein and the new reorganization plan. Icahn is supporting the old plan. Icahn is therefore supporting Ben LeBow. And Ben LeBow needs Icahn's support. Finally, in November 1994, LeBow and Icahn triumph together: A U.S. bankruptcy court approved New Valley's reorganization plan, allowing it to emerge from Chapter 11 by early 1995. The company will pay Class A shareholders a $50-a-share cash dividend. You'll be stunned by Icahn's "catch" for his bonds after two and a half years: a cool $150 million!

Is LeBow finally rid of Icahn? Of course not. Icahn now admits that he has been accumulating shares of Brooke group, the controlling shareholder of the reorganized New Valley. And who controls Brooke? None other than LeBow. So the LeBow-Icahn infighting will continue. Another yachting vacation in the Mediterranean may be in the works.

Honesty: Is It the Best Policy After All?

Thus far the Wall Street money managers encountered in this book are just about unanimous in succumbing to the temptations to engage in insider trading that is an inherent part of their job. Other money managers introduced in later chapters will also partake. The prohibitions against insider trading are honored mainly in the breach, as Hamlet would say, but there are exceptions to the rule, and these relatively rare individuals should be honored too.

A case in point is "Mona Larramie." This is one instance in which I wish I could use this woman's actual name, but circumstances don't allow it. It also follows that the name I shall use for her investment management firm, "Mona Capital Management Co.," has been modified accordingly.

Mona Capital shepherds about $200 million in assets of select individuals and smaller institutions. It's a small firm by Wall Street standards, and the plain truth is that it will probably stay that way, given Mona's sense of integrity. It's tough if not impossible to play by the rules on Wall Street and reach the very top. We shall see in this story how her no-nonsense work and integrity cost her valuable clients and a lot of money—$60 million in assets to be exact, a very significant loss for a smallish company.

The story begins one morning when one of Mona's associates, "Barbara Bache" (a pseudonym, of course), burst into her boss's office flush with excitement about information that had been imparted at a breakfast meeting with one of the firm's major clients. Barbara is a serene woman most of the time. This was highly unusual behavior for her. And yes, when she had finally calmed down, she indicated that the information imparted during the breakfast meeting was on the order of "well, kind of 'inside' information."

"Please don't tell me about it," Mona said instantly. "And don't spill it to anybody else."

The most amazing thing about Mona's reaction was that she *wasn't even curious*. She knows that reams of inside information make the rounds on Wall Street every working day, and she simply takes no part in it. She wants nothing to do with anything even remotely tainted by illegality. Therefore, she dismissed this "offer" without a second thought. She even got slightly angry at Barbara for putting her in a position where she had to say no.

Barbara's information concerned "Knickerbocker Enterprises," a chain of apparel stores for men and women in which Mona Capital maintained a considerable position for all of its clients: 4 million shares total but less than 5 percent of the shares outstanding. Mona had this confidence in spite of persistent rumors in the retailing industry that Knickerbocker was having trouble with its suppliers. Mona's analyst dismissed those concerns. At his suggestion, Mona had bought into the company early in 1992 at $9, and a year later the stock was approaching $18. The analyst was proud of that pick, and Mona was thankful too, because 1992 had been a difficult year all in all.

But by mid-1993, the stock had begun to wobble. Speculation swirled regarding merchandising and financing problems. By autumn the stock was looking really soggy—it had given back every point it had risen since early in 1992—and Mona called in her analyst for another conference. He remained optimistic. His numbers checked out. He was convinced they should hold on to Knickerbocker and wait for the next rally.

Mona Capital had always followed a long-term investing strategy: Stay with good companies and good stocks for the long haul. This approach went hand in hand with Mona's lack of interest in dealing with insider information, which is usually designed to yield short-term bonanzas. But there was that almost 100 percent profit she could have taken when the stock was at $17, when rumors were already circulating. Mona could hardly set aside her concerns, but her analyst assured her that there was no truth to the rumors.

On November 11, 1993, the situation became even more ominous for Mona when Knickerbocker announced that it might soon report a modest operating loss for the third quarter. The stock slipped down to the range of $4 to $5. Then the bad news about the operating loss was topped by a report in *The New York Times* that certain companies and credit-rating agencies were advising against further shipments to the suddenly beleaguered Knickerbocker. Company executives countered that they had been paying their bills on time and would continue to do so.

When she read the story in the *Times*, Mona felt a jab in her gut. True to her principles, she and Barbara had not spoken a word about the information conveyed weeks earlier at the breakfast meeting, but she had a very strong suspicion that it must have concerned Knickerbocker, that it had been an advance warning of impending doom. Mona called in Barbara and asked her whether this was the case.

"I wanted to tell you," Barbara replied, "but I respected your position."

"Well, tell me now," Mona said. Obviously the news was no longer tainted. The market had spoken.

Barbara confirmed Mona's worst fears: The client had verified the cash problems at Knickerbocker, and the company was having trouble paying its suppliers. Mona's client knew this because his brother was a senior executive at one of the suppliers which had threatened to stop shipments unless overdue bills were paid.

"Careful how you handle this," the client had told Barbara in effect, "because I don't want your information to be traced back to me and my brother, but I urge Mona Capital to get out of the stock *now*." Of course, this investor respected Mona's integrity—all her clients did; that was one reason why they were her clients—but this investor also considered Mona to be a *pragmatic* money manager. Pragmatic money managers do what's necessary.

Mona sat at her desk staring into space. *Four million shares.* Then she got angry not with Barbara but with Knickerbocker for not playing straight with her and with her analyst, for blowing it. In fact, this man was looking for a new job by the following afternoon.

The Knickerbocker fiasco pulled down Mona Capital's performance in 1993—she sold at $3½—although it still outperformed the Dow and S&P indexes. This was a small consolation. The year was a mark against a tradition of lofty performances at Mona Capital. In addition, two major clients fired Mona Capital because of the large exposure and costly loss in Knickerbocker. That was $40 million in assets. Subsequently, two other clients pulled out $10 million each.

In 1994 Knickerbocker filed for Chapter 11 and announced that it would close more stores in addition to the 200 already shuttered. About 100 full-time employees would lose their jobs. Later in the year it reported second-quarter losses of $40 million, or 70 cents a share, on sales that were down 18 percent to $176 million.

And the stock? It was long gone, trading at $1¾.

Without a doubt Mona was bitter about the whole experience, but she refuses to change her policy on insider trading. She just won't do it. "I am what I am," she told me. "I can't change that part of me."

But she did change her analysis policies. First, Barbara was promoted to the position of portfolio manager–analyst.

But Mona doesn't take Barbara's word for everything. She doesn't take any analyst's word as final. She now personally visits with the management of every company Mona Capital invests in. With her scruples against insider trading, Mona acknowledges that she and her team have to be "1,000 percent in the money and on the ball."

Occasionally a money manager is offered straight cash in exchange for illegal trading … and occasionally he or she turns it down. "Thomas Moore," a respected manager who opened his own shop in 1992 with assets of $200 million, did just that early in his career, in 1970. Just twenty-five years old at that time, Moore had bagged a promising job as a portfolio manager at one of the top performing funds in the business, the "Amherst Fund," which had assets of $120 million. That kind of money made Amherst a major player in the go-go era, just when stocks and funds were beginning to break out of a long lethargy. Moore's young neck and reputation were on the line, and he knew it. What he didn't know was that his entire future in the securities business was about to be on the line too.

One afternoon Moore took a call from a man I shall call "Steve Parsons," a financial executive of "Techton Corp.," a large industrial company. Techton was a major client of the Amherst Fund. Parsons was therefore an important contact for Moore, and the older man yucked it up with Moore over the phone during their general discussion of his company's stake in the Amherst Fund and Amherst's plans for the future. Three days later Parsons called with a lunch invitation. Again, this was not an offer Moore could refuse—and why would he have wanted to? Parsons was an important man for the Amherst Fund. Moore jumped at the invitation to lunch. He might even have purchased a new tie for the occasion.

The two men met at Delmonico's, a Wall Street hangout and restaurant (now closed) that pops up occasionally in these pages. If the SEC could only obtain a recording of every luncheon conversation at Delmonico's....

Anyway, Moore was somewhat surprised to find himself enjoying Parsons's company. A squat, balding smoker of cigars, he was also pleasant, frank, and confident. And he was bringing Moore good news. Parsons was about to boost his company's participation in the Amherst Fund from $10 million to $20 million. This would be a tremendous coup for Moore if any of the credit for the new money managed to go to him. He grabbed the lunch check from Steve Parsons's hand. The fund would be glad to take care of it, including the $50 for their drinks alone. Parsons had poured down five double martinis in the course of the nearly three-hour lunch.

A week later Parsons was back on the phone to Moore, inviting him to Techton's offices on the Avenue of the Americas to discuss the company's additional $10 million investment. After proudly displaying the breathtaking view of Manhattan through the floor-to-ceiling windows, Parsons got immediately to the point. He said, "You know, Tom"— already the informal "Tom"—"I own a lot of stock in

Techton. About $2 million worth if I include all my stock options."

Moore was puzzled. What was the point of this information? He asked Parsons, who glanced at the door to be certain it was closed before continuing the conversation.

"I have a favor to ask," Parsons then blurted it out.

Moore stared in amazement as the executive of this well-known company then asked this twenty-five-year-old money manager at the Amherst Fund to buy shares of Techton for that fund. Parsons knew that if a respected fund like Amherst moved into Techton, the purchase would attract interest on the Street. The stock would spike *quickly,* and Parsons would move *quietly* to cash in.

"Buy a big bunch of them—as much as your funds can afford and will allow."

Moore was speechless. He couldn't believe what he was hearing. There were any number of *quid pro quos* hidden in his request. Parsons had made clear that his stake in the company would benefit enormously if Moore would make this purchase. His position as an investor in the Amherst Fund gave considerable weight to the "request." This wasn't just unethical, Moore thought. It's illegal.

Then came the clincher: "I'll pay you $50,000. Cash."

Moore stood up and shouted, "That's outrageous and that's illegal, for God's sake," and walked out of the office. He was young, but he knew what the repercussions of his refusal would be, and exactly two weeks later the letter arrived. The executive at Techton requested that the fund redeem half its $10 million stake. One month later he requested redemption of the other half. Moore never had another thing to do with Steve Parsons.

He was truly agitated. He knew that he had done the right thing in rejecting the bribe, but he had cost the firm a big account. Would he get the ax? He would not. When he explained to his superiors what had happened, he received 100 percent support for his decision. Indeed, it's rare that insider trading on the Street involves the actual passing of cash in envelopes. Many of the insiders who will gladly take a tainted profit in the market and rationalize that profit as shrewdness would balk at the idea of accepting $50,000 in crisp new bills. That's too close to pure thievery. (But it happens, as when Marty Siegel accepted $900,000 in crisp new bills from Ivan Boesky.)

The Analyst's Cushy Couch

N otice anything in common regarding many of the money managers who played key roles in the preceding chapters? Carl Smith, the Iranian's old friend who got almost whipsawed with Midwest Oil, started out in the business as an analyst. Max Rosenthal got his feet wet as an analyst. And Jerry without a last name who walked out on Max to form his own venture began life as an analyst at a major Wall Street firm before moving on to a competitor.

Sometimes it seems that almost all the movers and shakers on the Street are former analysts. Those who aren't former analysts are *still* analysts. But don't feel sorry for these hardworking souls. The best command salaries in the high six figures, sometimes even seven, and they too can do quite well when it comes to insider trading.

Like their "colleagues" in psychotherapy, the members of the fraternity/sorority of Wall Street security analysts know just about all there is to know about their patients. In fact, who would know more about a company than an analyst who spends days and weeks studying its operations? Only its top management—and the analyst knows those men and women pretty well too.

On the word of the analysts hangs the fate of the stock. Even if their estimates on sales and earnings aren't quite gospel, they're the closest thing to it on this earth. When the world of commerce needs to put a value on a company and its stock, it turns to this cadre of critics, who pull their numbers from a hat as skillfully as any magician. And those numbers translate quite nicely into real greenbacks for themselves, their clients, the companies in question, and smart investors.

Like the opinions of New York's food critics, which make or break restaurants every week, the judgments of analysts can fatten or flatten a stock, no questions asked. Woe to a company that fails to meet the analysts' expectations. This stock will probably head due south the day after the release of the quarterly report. This is especially true in the context of a generally uncertain market in which some investors are looking for an excuse to bail out. When a stock gets a rave from an analyst, especially from one of the stars at a major Wall Street house, that's a guaranteed spike of a point or two, minimum, the very moment the rave hits the broadtape, as the Dow Jones News Wire is called.

The analysts occupy the catbird seat. Not only do they have an intimate knowledge of the company and a direct line to the CEO. Not only are they in a position to acquire and be given all sorts of inside information. Best of all, they are uniquely positioned to generate *their own* inside information. For example, would an analyst ever sell his or her inside information—for example, the nature of his or her upcoming assessment—to interested bystanders, including the management of the company in question? It's been known to happen.

More common is the particular type of insider trading called front-running, which is simplicity itself. Say the analyst is prepared to issue a very positive report on UFO Corp. First the analyst buys a judicious number of shares for his or her own portfolio, prepared to cash in on the upcoming spike generated by his or her own report. Or say the analyst is prepared to pan XYZ Corp. First the analyst sells short, ready to buy in a couple of days when the stock dips a few points. Would an analyst ever connive with his or her own brokerage house or investment company to load up on a stock that was about to receive a highly positive recommendation? Big-time institutional front-running? It's been known to happen.

Naturally, caution is required in all these circumstances. These front-running tricks are simple, but they're also obvious—to the boss if he or she is not involved and to the regulators.

Don't get me wrong. Most analysts are honest practitioners of their arcane trade. They're paid well enough that they don't need to manipulate reports to their own advantage. But some analysts don't have such scruples. Front-running happens every day on Wall Street, but it's often disguised. The analyst doesn't trade for his or her own account. He or she works through a best friend, a brother-in-law, a husband, a lover. It's almost impossible for regulators to impede these tactics.

Blatant front-running aside, security analysts are very much part of that network of incestuous relationships that yield handsome profits on Wall Street. The story of the man I shall call "Vinnie DeVito" is a perfect illustration. The Italian pseudonym is intentional because Vinnie is an Italian guy who grew up in Brooklyn, but not in one of the Italian neighborhoods in that borough. It was in one of the Jewish neighborhoods, where his gregarious personality earned him the description "spinmeister." Some of his Jewish friends have upped the ante and still call him "the Roman spinmeister," honoring both his Italian heritage and his enviable ability to put an interesting spin on any story.

After earning his undergraduate degree in business and an MBA, Vinnie encountered few difficulties moving from his first job as a backroom clerk at a small brokerage firm, to a stockbroker at a mid-sized firm, to an analyst at one of the top firms on the Street, and finally to a major industry analyst at another major Wall Street investment bank. This was in 1982. (Spinmeistering comes in handy on Wall Street too, where well-placed friends are all important and captivating storytelling is a prime way to make those friends.)

In this elite position, Vinnie was in his element. The spinmeister became bosom buddies with many of the CEOs in the drug industry. Top brass throughout that industry were his friends. Vinnie was on a "first call" basis with everyone who was anyone in pharmaceuticals. Not only could he tell a story, he was a good listener too, and he became privy to all manner of "insidy" information on the private lives of top management.

In 1988, Vinnie received a call from "Richard Roosevelt," who was at that time the chairman and CEO of "Pharmco Group," a major distributor of prescription and over-the-counter medicines. Roosevelt and Vinnie were particularly close, and Roosevelt had just one question: Why was Pharmco's stock moving up so strongly? Was something going on that the CEO himself didn't know about? (By the way, this story is unrelated to the Pharmco episode involving hedge fund titan Max Rosenthal that I related in a preceding chapter. That episode happened two years prior to this. However, Richard Roosevelt was the Pharmco CEO both times.)

Vinnie knew that something was indeed going on, for a fact. He knew that Pharmco was considered a vulnerable takeover target in those go-go days of leveraged buyouts. But now Vinnie thought, If the chairman of the company is calling me out of the blue asking for information, how serious could the rumored takeover be? No deal was in the making, at least not yet. Vinnie was certain of this. He saw no good reason for his friend the CEO to be calling around if a deal was in the works. Such calls would just focus Vinnie's attention on the stock and the rumored takeover. Roosevelt was much too smart to do that. Nor did Vinnie think his friend

would play a trick on him by pretending to be in the dark
when he was actually in the know. Again, Roosevelt was too
smart for that kind of trick, which could backfire.

Vinnie told Roosevelt that he would check with his sources
to try to find out what was happening with the stock, and
that was what he did. He found out who was fueling the
takeover rumors, and his search didn't take long. Over a couple of drinks in the fern bar around the corner from Vinnie's
office, a secretary at one of Pharmco's competitors told
Vinnie that her company was poised to make a play for
Pharmco. This woman had gotten the word from a friend
who was one of the portfolio managers for the company's
pension fund and who had said that the fund was buying
Pharmco heavily for just that reason. Vinnie was not surprised at this news. He had heard that a "conglomerate" was
eyeballing Pharmco, and this company fit that description.

Just as Vinnie was getting this "information" (on Wall
Street a rumor is information of a sort), Pharmco's stock
was popping. In two days it jumped 8 points. This could
only mean that the takeover speculation was widespread
and growing. Vinnie had to decide whether to jump on this
bandwagon and urge his people to buy the stock, and he had
to decide quickly.

His move was to go against the market and short the
stock at this higher price! Vinnie was convinced that
Roosevelt's phone call meant that there was no deal for
Pharmco in the making. This rumor was just that and nothing more, and it would have a very short life, he was certain. And when this rumor burst, Pharmco's stock would

give back those 8 points and maybe more. Vinnie was betting on it.

His bold bet proved accurate. Pharmco Group issued a statement that it was not in talks with another company, and Pharmco Group stock plunged more than 10 points in three days. From the outside, that decision to go short might have looked like an easy win for Vinnie, but it wasn't. It took nerve and astute judgment to go against a strong rumor that the market was taking seriously. It also took his close relationship with Richard Roosevelt, which had led the CEO to consult with Vinnie.

Roosevelt's phone call to Vinnie was not illegal, and Vinnie's deduction was *not* out of bounds or a violation of any securities law. A great deal of what we might call the exchange of inside information is perfectly legal, and so is any subsequent trading on the basis of that information.

A year later Pharmco's stock began acting up again. This time around the speculation that came Vinnie's way centered on a European bank bidding for Pharmco shares on behalf of unidentified clients. Vinnie called Richard Roosevelt, and something strange happened, something very strange. Throughout their long friendship the two men had felt free to call each other anytime, anyplace, and that call always got through. Roosevelt had even called Vinnie from his company's boardroom during a board meeting, seeking specific information from his favorite analyst. But now, for the first time ever, Roosevelt was unavailable. His secretary

told Vinnie that Roosevelt was in conference with a delega-
tion from out of town.

But that circumstance had never stopped Roosevelt from
taking a call from Vinnie. Coincidence? Vinnie didn't think
so. This turn of events could only mean one thing. The
unanswered phone call meant that something was indeed
going on. Roosevelt must have felt that he had to be secre-
tive about it with his old friend the analyst. Rather than risk
a leak by informing Vinnie of the big news, rather than
deceive him with some kind of half-truth, he would say
nothing at all.

What could be going on? It had to be big for Roosevelt
to handle it that way. Vinnie was sure of it. In fact, he was
sure a takeover might really be cooking. Any one of the
major European chemical or pharmaceutical companies was
a good possibility, he thought. The deal might even be
already done and ready to come out of the oven.

With absolutely no time to waste, Vinnie swung into
action, *buying* Pharmco shares at $42, then $43, and finally
$44. Queries started coming in about Pharmco Group. The
stock kept climbing: Within a week it had reached $49. But
the day after it reached that point, the ubiquitous financial
columnist and broadcaster Dan Dorfman mentioned
Pharmco Group on his midday television show. Dorfman
stated that one of his sources strongly believed that there
wasn't an iota of truth in the latest, fresh rumors that
Pharmco was high on everybody's takeover list.

The stock plunged back to the low $40s, then to $40,
then down to the mid-$30s. Vinnie watched the tape all the

way, but he held fast to his shares. He knew that Dorfman
had been correct many times in the past and would probably be correct many times in the future, but Vinnie had
absolute trust in his relationship with Richard Roosevelt.
Vinnie was confident that he understood the hidden
message behind that unanswered phone call to the CEO,
especially when it *remained* unanswered throughout the following weeks. This was just totally at odds with his longstanding relationship with Roosevelt. Something big was
going on. Vinnie was convinced that Dorfman had been
given a bum steer by investors shorting the stock.

Vinnie continued to go the other way. He bought even
more shares of Pharmco Group, a lot more. He purchased
call options, betting that the stock would rise all the way to
$60. Given the market, that was a very aggressive play. But
Vinnie had revisited all the numbers and had specifically
rethought the possibility of a move by one of the European
conglomerates. He was one of the few analysts on this side
of the Atlantic who followed the company closely. He
thought he knew the thinking of this company's management, and he thought they were more than casually interested in Pharmco.

Plus he had someone inside the company. That always
helps.

Her name was "Veronique," a young marketing executive
regarded as something of a whiz kid because of her quick
wit and knowledge of the global economy and the political
temper of the Group of Seven. Vinnie had met her five
years earlier, literally bumping into her in the elevator in the

building in New York where this company maintained an office. Brief introductions revealed common interests in the drug industry and the science of chemistry, which Vinnie had enjoyed in college. Veronique and Vinnie had maintained a casual friendship for the five years before the day he called her about the takeover rumors.

Veronique anticipated the line of questioning. She told Vinnie about an asset evaluation of Pharmco she had seen in her offices. The numbers were $60 to $80 per share.

Vinnie put down the phone and bought more stock. Four months later: bull's-eye. Pharmco Group had moved toward $90. Then in 1990, the European company acquired a majority stake in Pharmco for more than $100 a share and subsequently merged the firm into its own pharmaceutical division.

Vinnie invited Veronique for a much deserved celebration at the Rainbow Room. There is no question that he had illegally traded on her inside tip, but he had made the correct analysis of the situation even before that in the case of the unanswered phone call. Roosevelt went on to become the Chairman and CEO of the combined entities, the company formed through the merger of the Pharmco Group with the division of this European company.

Every Man for Himself

Once a securities analyst, always a securities analyst. The habit of reading between the lines of quarterly reports and press releases stays with an analyst long after he or she may have moved into another position on Wall Street. One reason so many major players on the Street have been analysts at one time is that those skills are valuable wherever a person ends up.

Also valuable and highly "transportable" are the friendships established and cultivated by an analyst. A shrewd analyst maintains these friendships long after moving on to greener pastures, because he or she never knows when they may be needed. A case in point is one "Tony Conti," as I shall refer to him. At the time our story begins, Tony is one of the younger junior partners at a top Wall Street investment bank, which shall remain unspecified. Conti had the reputation at this prestigious investment bank of being a highly pragmatic analyst and a plucky stock picker. Before earning that coveted partnership at his firm, Conti had been one of the Street's top-ranked industry analysts. He had been in the industry for fifteen years, knew his business inside and out, and commanded the respect of the top exec-utives. Now his knowledge and his connections continued to serve him well.

One mid-December weekend in 1985, Tony was at his oceanfront home in Florida, where he went as often as pos-sible to get away from the harshness of life in New York—not that things were all that harsh at his six-bedroom home in Westchester County, that charming enclave north of New York City where many of the Street's big hitters main-tain homes. Both of his residences were a long way from the Italian neighborhood in the Bronx where Tony grew up. His parents still didn't have a really clear idea of their son's busi-ness, but whatever it was that he did down on Wall Street, the rewards it brought to him and to them were easy enough to see.

Early that morning, Tony woke up expecting to enjoy a day at the beach with his wife and two sons. Then he turned on the early-morning CNN broadcast and saw pictures of the explosion at the Union Carbide plant in Bhopal, India. Tony almost dropped his cup of coffee, and he had to admit later that his first concern had little to do with the tragic loss of lives in distant Bhopal. The carnage in Tony's mind was all the red ink in his bank account. His mind raced ahead to an image of Union Carbide's collapsing stock price on the Big Board. Carbide had been a high flier for several weeks, chalking up big gains for Tony and his clients. He still had a buy recommendation on the company.

Maybe the CNN report was wrong! Tony jumped from the couch and ran to the porch to retrieve the morning papers. But all of them, including *The Wall Street Journal*, reported the same fact: It was a Union Carbide plant. Tony cursed. The thought sped through his mind that he should have paid cash for this beach house when he had had the money to pay. Now who knew what might happen on the market? Tony even had a quick thought of getting totally wiped out, but he shut out this nightmare as quickly as it came. Perhaps his fear of potential losses was exaggerated, but a significant percentage of his assets was tied up in Union Carbide, and a number of his clients were also invested heavily in that stock. This explosion was bad news.

But what made matters even worse for Tony Conti was that he had been "inside" on one of the best kept secrets on Wall Street at that time. And this secret was about Carbide. Just a week before the explosion in Bhopal, Carbide's chairman, Warren Anderson, had been deep in negotiations with his counterparts at Atlantic Richfield. The talks had made a good deal of progress, and an agreement to sell Union Carbide's petrochemical division to ARCO for a cool $3.5 billion was close at hand. The sale would be a coup for Carbide. The division had been a money loser for some time, and few analysts on the Street would have put that kind of price on the property. However, ARCO had gotten wind of the fact that operations at the plant had turned around. They thought they could make it perform at the $3.5 billion price.

However, Tony wasn't the only one who had gotten an inside position on this sale. Others in the market must have gotten wind of the rumors that Carbide was attempting a restructuring of its assets. The Friday before the Bhopal accident, the stock had traded in the mid-$50s.

By the week after the explosion Carbide had plunged to $29. Tony and his clients had taken a heavy hit, on paper, at least. Tony was not happy. The panic about being wiped out had passed, but Tony was still mad about his lousy luck. A great piece of inside action had been blown away by the explosion.

Then the incredible happened. The stock reversed direction and began inching up. The world wasn't about to collapse. Carbide was alive and kicking. "There is a God after all!" Tony shouted as he watched the tape.

But why the market's change of mind on Carbide? This spike seemed to Tony like more than the predictable minirebound that usually follows a tragedy-related plunge. He started digging. He called all the friends he had gathered in the chemical industry over fifteen years and found out that there was an explanation very different from the simple mini-rebound.

The big boys were moving in on Carbide. Tony had it from an impeccable source on the trading floor that the billionaire Bass brothers from Fort Worth, Texas, were coming in about as fast as they could at $29 to $30 a share on the advice of their most insightful investment strategist, Richard Rainwater. What's more, another mole on the grapevine assured Tony that none other than hedge funder Mike Steinhardt had also moved in on Carbide.

To Tony, these investors were just verifying his own thinking. Yes, the preliminary estimates projected a $1 billion loss for Carbide on the Bhopal explosion, but Tony knew for a fact, practically, that the firm was about to receive a check for $3.5 billion from ARCO. And psychologically, it seemed, the market was ready to put the cost of the explosion in perspective. Tony placed big orders for his own portfolio and those of his valued clients.

Sure enough, the Bass family soon filed the 13D form with the Securities and Exchange Commission, acknowledging that they had acquired more than 5 percent of Carbide's stock. (The figure eventually climbed to 7.8 percent.) The reaction to this news by the top echelon of Carbide was mixed. Chairman Anderson pooh-poohed the Basses' interest, claiming that he saw nothing sinister. In fact, he interpreted it as a shrewd investment on the part of shrewd investors who agreed with him that the company had tremendous assets and was undervalued in the market, regardless of the Bhopal tragedy. Anderson assured everyone that he had only respect for those brothers out west in Cowtown, U.S.A.

But Carbide's president, Al Flamm, sized matters up much differently. Flamm was grim. He smelled a takeover, and if Carbide was so undervalued, it was a perfect target. He thought the Basses were bad news. Flamm had respect for his friend Tony Conti, and Tony had been telling him about takeover talk and had even added another name to the growing list of possible raiders: Samuel Heyman, the predatory, always-prowling Chairman of GAF Inc., the specialty chemical company, of which he had acquired control through a hostile takover battle some years before.

Tony and Flamm discussed the Union Carbide situation directly. Tony and Anderson did not. They did not like each other, an unusual animosity in Tony's case, since he was such a friendly and likable guy.

Tony agreed with Flamm that Carbide was red meat for the raiders. Several weeks after the Basses had filed their 13D form with the SEC, GAF Inc. filed its own form! Now it too owned at least 5 percent of Carbide. And Heyman had also been building up a sizable position in the stock for his personal portfolio.

The GAF-Heyman filing with the SEC sent Carbide stock soaring. Within days it jumped from the mid-$30s to $45. Just months after the tragic explosion Bhopal was a distant and irrelevant memory on Wall Street. When things quieted down, the Bass brothers made their move, pulling their money from Carbide stock—but not before offering Carbide's management an opportunity to buy back the stake. This sounded very much like greenmail, in which a large investor pressures management to buy back shares to avert a hostile takeover attempt. Carbide's management said no thank you.

Within *half an hour,* that huge block of stock ended up in the hands of Samuel Heyman's group, and with a nice premium for the Basses. The news electrified the Street, and shares jumped to $50 instantaneously. The Street's army of arbitrageurs thought that the Heyman group must now feel confident about going full-bore for Union Carbide, that world-renowned but troubled giant of the chemical industry. Why else would Heyman pay the Basses a nice premium for their block of shares? He wasn't in the habit of showing such generosity for no reason. Carbide was in play now certainly, ripe for the picking in that era of superbuyouts and megamergers when hundreds of millions of dollars were made literally overnight. The market saw Union Carbide as its next big profit center.

But was it correct? The pressure was on Tony Conti to find out. At the same time, he received a phone call from Bob Freeman, the chief arbitrageur at Goldman, Sachs. Freeman knew him to be an extremely knowledgeable analyst. He also knew Tony could be pugnacious, but he would have to deal with that because he needed Tony's input. That's what arbitrage is all about: good information, then better information, and then, finally, *perfect* information.

On the phone, Freeman got right to business: "What do you think of this Heyman thing, Tony? Tell me what you know."

Sure enough, Conti was insulted by the peremptory tone. A seasoned veteran of Wall Street, he didn't like being ordered around by Bob Freeman, no matter how tall and domineering he was or how big a cheese he happened to be at Goldman, Sachs. Tony didn't feel he was anybody's minion. He knew the answer to Freeman's question—Heyman wanted Carbide badly—but was damned if he was going to give this arb the inside scoop. He told the other man bluntly that he and everyone else had blown it when Tony had said months earlier that Carbide was a $60 stock and no one had cared to listen.

"Sorry, babe," Tony stated, and with that remark he hung up the telephone. That evening over dinner at Chiam, Tony's favorite Chinese restaurant in the city, he looked to his wife for commiseration. He wasn't going to hand over the inside information. The guy just wouldn't get it, the pighead. Tony wouldn't tell the big lug. The derogatory names were spilling out as Conti built up a head of steam for what he assumed would be another confrontation when Freeman called again.

To his surprise, it never happened. Freeman never called, and now this new *silence* got Conti to pondering the situation. Had Freeman found out what he needed to know from another source? Yes. One of Tony's pals revealed that Freeman had been buying Carbide like crazy.

"He was buying like he had found the perfect information," the trader said. "And you know what, Tony? Freeman did find the Holy Grail this time."

Conti gulped.

The trader went on to explain that the local golden boy had found out that none other than Ivan Boesky, the maestro of all arbs, had been buying heavily. In his heyday Boesky had tremendous clout on Wall Street. He was in a position to generate the large commission fees that fed the partnerships at the big brokerage houses. Therefore, he invariably was the first to receive the best information on deals being hatched anywhere in the country. The arb community stood in awe of Boesky. When he bought, they bought. So Freeman bought.

But exactly how had Freeman learned this information about Boesky and Union Carbide? The trader did not know.

In fact, Freeman's deep throat was Martin Siegel, the mergers and acquisitions chief at Kidder Peabody. Nobody knew this at that time, but Siegel and Boesky had already established the very cozy relationship that would get both of them arrested and land Boesky in prison. Simply put, Siegel gave Boesky the inside scoop on deals Siegel was working on. It was a case of flagrant abuse of inside information.

Specifically in this instance, Siegel knew about the Heyman play for Union Carbide because he and Heyman lived in the same bedroom community of Westport, Connecticut, and Siegel often joined Heyman to fly into work in Manhattan on the GAF helicopter. Therefore, Heyman felt very comfortable hiring Kidder Peabody to be the investment bank for GAF in the move against Carbide. And since Siegel was chief of that mergers and acquisitions department, he had perfect information on the deal, which he passed along to Boesky—for a fee, of course. (As it turned out, Siegel's link with Boesky was the crime that led to the downfall of both men. Boesky acknowledged receiving inside information on certain takeover transactions, and

Siegel admitted to delivering some of that information. One of his payoffs was the $900,000 in cash delivered in an attaché case by a Boesky courier.)

Meanwhile, Union Carbide's top management was not asleep as the takeover rumors built momentum and the arbs jostled for position. The executives would not go down without a fight. As one of a series of moves designed to thwart a hostile takeover, management decided to spin off the battery division with a book value that was estimated to be worth $33 a share in Carbide stock. This maneuver catapulted Carbide stock to as high as $105.

Heyman had acquired his stake for an average of $50, and so he had scored a paper profit of about $450 million. The firm and all its clients might have enjoyed an even larger windfall because they owned shares in both Carbide and GAF. Tony Conti was also as happy as could be. After all, he had been buying back when the stock had been selling in the $30s.

What happened next? The battle seemed to become frozen in limbo. Heyman had the huge paper profits on the Carbide stock, but if GAF pulled off the takeover, its own stock, selling for $10 at the time, would also fly all the way to the moon. Therefore, most analysts on the Street thought that Heyman would go for broke and make the move. Tony was not one of them. He took his profits. He was right, many others were wrong. One morning everything just fell apart. Heyman pulled the plug on the Union Carbide merry-go-round. GAF would no longer pursue the company. Although GAF stock tumbled more than 50 percent, to $4,

Heyman had made a huge personal pile from the meteoric ascent of Carbide's stock.

Immediately after the electricity went out of the deal, Carbide fell to $45, where it languished for some time before management restructured and sold some assets. Tony Conti lost some paper profit when the stock skidded, but he was able to get out with plenty of real profit. All the major players did.

Painting the Tape

lthough securities analysts like Vinnie DeVito and the legion of former analysts like Tony Conti are nicely positioned for the inside play on the market, they do not have final "hands-on" control of the buying and selling of stocks. With the exception of "private placement" deals between very large investors (such as the Bass-to-Heyman sale at the end of the Union Carbide caper), orders to buy and sell stocks go through traders from brokers. Traders in turn have to move their orders to their "floor brokers" on the floor of the exchange. These floor brokers then go to the "specialists" posted on the floor of the New York and American exchanges. Therefore, it is the specialist who has the final say about which orders do and do not get bought and sold. Despite what casual Wall Street investors might believe, this transaction is *not* automatic. The specialist has to make it happen.

Therefore, the specialist is *always* ahead of the investing crowd, by definition, because almost every buy and sell order has to cross his or her desk and be entered in the ledger. Talk about inside action! *That's* the ultimate inside action, and shrewd specialists know how to cash it in. Of course, you would not expect specialists to buy space in *The Wall Street Journal* to advertise their surefire, cast-iron edge in the market, and they don't. In fact, they're notorious for moaning and groaning about their hectic days and heavy losses on the trading floor. But don't believe a word of it. For them, the stock exchange is a playground and they're the big kid on the block. Stocks are toys to manipulate and cash in on. The real truth is that there's no way for a specialist to lose in this game, no way whatsoever. Let's see why.

On the New York and American exchanges, specialists are either self-employed or work for a firm that is authorized by the exchange to specialize in certain stocks. Either way, the specialist is not an employee of the exchange. One specialist is in charge of anywhere between ten and forty different stocks. For these stocks, the specialist is in effect the brokers' broker. When a broker on the floor receives an order to sell XYZ Corp. at a specific price—a "limit order," as it is called—he or she can hardly be expected to wait around the specialists' post until the stock rises to that price. The broker will leave the order with the specialist, who will then enter it into his or her little black book (a computer, actually), the complete record of all buy and sell orders as well as an inventory of his or her holdings in the stock. When and if XYZ reaches that price, the specialist must execute that limit order.

The result of this system is that the specialist has no need to guess what the market is going to be doing in the near future. The specialist *knows* because he or she has a record of the limit orders right there. Specialists *are* the market in the near future. Now, it doesn't require Einstein's mind to suspect that such foreknowledge and hands-on control of the market for a particular stock are tantamount to being given the key to the bank. Just as the securities analyst of XYZ Corp. is in the best position to learn what's going on inside the company's operations, the specialist for XYZ stock is in the best position to know what's going on with the company's stock. Plus the specialist will certainly culti-vate the same friendships with XYZ management that the analyst cultivates.

Presto! The specialist has the best of both worlds: the inside scoop on operations and the advance scoop on mar-ket activity.

Bottom line: The brokers' broker is the insiders' insider.

While serving in this envied capacity, the specialist is also charged with maintaining an orderly market for the issues he or she is assigned.

Orderly market. That's the phrase that's always used. Simply put, the specialist is supposed to keep things from going haywire. The straightforward way to accomplish this is to maintain a fluid balance between supply and demand so that prices move up and down at a moderate pace. The specialist must be a stabilizing force by bridging temporary gaps between supply and demand.

The mechanism is simple. When supply in the market greatly exceeds demand, the specialist must artificially boost demand by buying shares for his or her inventory. Similarly, when supply is low and demand is great, the specialist must sell shares from that inventory. If the specialist does not have those shares in his or her portfolio, he or she may have to borrow shares–short selling–to make up the shortage.

In the beehive which is the stock exchange floor, the specialist is the queen bee herself. Incredible investment opportunities can open up and close again within a matter of not minutes but seconds. Who's better positioned than the specialist to capitalize on these windows of opportunity? No one is, even though certain rules of the exchange place restrictions on these activities. For example, the specialist cannot buy stock for his or her own account at a price at which he or she has previously agreed to execute a limit order. In other words, at any given price a specialist cannot buy for his or her own account *first*. Nor can a specialist arbitrarily raise the price of a stock if there is no bid outstanding at a price higher than the current price of the stock. This rule prevents the specialist from simply raising the price and, once a buyer comes in, selling stock from *his or her own* account for a guaranteed profit.

These are good rules, but they are not foolproof. Consider that age-old scam known on the Street as painting the tape. This is probably the most basic of all the scams in the specialist's bag of tricks. While the specialist's legitimate purpose is to bring order to the market, painting the tape is a way of *embellishing* it to the benefit of the seasoned and highly skilled specialist. This veteran of the exchange floor can elude the rules and create artificial activity in the stock, and this activity in turn captures the attention of cruising investors, who then rush in and push the price of the stock even higher. The net result is that the shares the specialist bought to create the artificial demand are now ripe for selling at a nifty profit as a result of that demand.

Of course, every specialist will deny, deny, deny that he or she has ever painted the tape, and perhaps he or she hasn't. There are some angels on Wall Street, but not all that many.

Specialists who acknowledge—off the record—that they have at least *heard of* painting the tape also insist that the practice doesn't really interfere with their legitimate function of establishing an orderly market. Perhaps so. But that excuse is about as convincing as the one offered by Jack Flaherty, the investment adviser—or bagman—who succeeded in getting the ball rolling on Medicure's stock, as was described in an earlier chapter. Flaherty defended his actions on the grounds that "nobody got hurt," but that is beside the point about insider trading, which is that not everyone has an equal opportunity to benefit.

The same principle applies here with painting the tape. Maybe there's no blood on the floor of the exchange as a result of a specialist's artistry, but the practice clearly works against the idea of equal chances and fair play. To show you how this works, I introduce "Sam Simon"—yet another pseudonym, I'm afraid, but I guarantee that no specialist will ever go on record by name to describe how he or she paints the tape.

Tall and thin, tan and trim, distinguished Sam Simon is always calm as he goes about his business on behalf of the free enterprise system. He keeps an immaculate book. He loves the power he wields over his corner at one of the major exchanges, where he has been a specialist for many years, working feverishly on behalf of the trusting American investor.

Here is Sam's account of the trading in Widget Co. shares in an unspecified year. Widget was trading at $10 at the time. Sam's inventory of the stock exceeded the demand by a large margin. It would be nice if he could unload some shares and make a little money, but how? By creating the demand himself.

Sam starts buying Widget in small but steady amounts, say, 3,000 to 5,000 shares, three, four, maybe five blocks within a period of several hours. Predictably, brokers start hounding him for information. Sam's pat response is, "Oh, one of my clients is buying." The next question is how "determined" this buyer is. They also ask what the specialist knows that they don't know. Sam plays it coy, naturally. "I think it's serious buying," he says. "This particular client is pretty smart. I'm also wondering what he's up to. But I respect his judgment. He's had a good streak lately."

Brokers ask Sam to sell them some Widget shares. Sam is cool to the idea. He only has 1,000 shares available, he says.

"What about at $10¼?"

"Maybe." Fifteen minutes later he satisfies an order for 2,000 shares at $10¼. Now a limit order comes in for 3,000 shares at $10¾. Sam is finally able to satisfy it. Eventually he gets most of his shares sold at $11, at which point he rations his remaining supply in order to sustain the price at the highest level.

This system works particularly well when Sam obtains some inside information from Widget headquarters. As a market veteran of long standing, he has friends in high places in all "his" companies. Say Sam has gotten wind of upcoming good news, news that will move the stock up. He makes certain he paints the tape pretty well in the two or three weeks before the news is announced. He carefully rations his supply of Widget shares and adds to this supply discreetly by buying for his own account. By the time the good news is official and the market is reacting in the upward direction, Sam will have disbursed his bloated inventory at ever higher prices.

If bad news was coming, Sam would short the stock in similar fashion.

Sam has to be careful, of course, and he is. He says he has never attracted the attention of the SEC or the stock exchange brass, and his profits have ballooned to multi-million-dollar levels. Therefore, Sam has plenty of cash for any tape-painting requirements that may come up.

But you ain't seen nothin' yet. If the opportunities for underhanded plays by the specialists on the New York and American exchanges seem too good to be true, the schemes pulled off by their counterparts on the Nasdaq over-the-counter (OTC) market are positively scandalous, especially since those schemes are perfectly legal!

The Nasdaq specialists are called market makers, and theirs is one of the most coveted jobs on Wall Street. The job really is a license to print money. The reason is simple enough. While a specialist on the New York and American exchanges is not allowed to arbitrarily jack up the asking price of one of his or her stocks, a Nasdaq market maker can do just that. This is why the gap between the buy and sell prices of many OTC stocks is often unreasonably large. On the Nasdaq exchange it's common to see a $10 bid and a $10⅝ asked. Such wide gaps are not allowed on the New York and American exchanges. That $10⅝ asked might well be the market maker's arbitrary and inflated number. You'll never know. If you decide to buy that stock at $10⅝, you'll never know whether you're giving the market maker a nice profit for his personal portfolio.

A somewhat more subtle but still common ploy by Nasdaq market makers is to manipulate the closing bid price at the end of the trading day for the benefit of favored traders with vulnerable margin accounts. This is a nifty maneuver available only to Nasdaq market makers and favored Nasdaq investors. It can't be done on the New York and American exchanges.

Here's how it works. A favored Nasdaq client has paid $50 per share for a substantial position in UFO Co., but thanks to his margin account, which is set at 50 percent, he has to put up only half the money, or $25 a share. As long as the stock stays at $50 or higher, this investor is safe from a margin call. But since the investor's debt cannot exceed 50 percent of the value of the stock, if the price falls below $50, the investor's brokerage house will require that he put up more money to maintain the 50 percent margin. For every $1 the price falls below $50, the investor has to put up 50 percent, or 50 cents.

At the end of this hypothetical working day on the market things are getting tight for the UFO investor: The trading price is in danger of dropping below the critical $50 mark. The market maker thinks that there's a definite possibility that some bids could come in as low as $48 and $49. If that occurs and if a seller accepts that bid, our most favored investor will receive a margin call, not a big one, granted, but a nuisance nonetheless. Besides, the market maker likes this investor, who has been known to pass along a tip or two. (Whether it's a literal or a figurative tip doesn't matter. Both are fungible on Wall Street.) He wants to help the investor out.

And he does so by arbitrarily setting the bid at $50 as the end of trading approaches. If it is accepted by a seller, he sets it at $50 one more time. Finally, the bell rings and the investor with the margin call is safe overnight. Nifty, and it happens, although these miracles are tougher to pull off with heavily traded stocks, where the volume on both the buying and selling sides will overwhelm any effort to control the price of the stock. But with more obscure issues like UFO, the shrewd and friendly market maker can handle the ball like Magic Johnson.

Do these machinations qualify as insider trading? It really doesn't matter, because the practice is perfectly legal on the OTC. None other than the Securities and Exchange

Commission itself acknowledged in a report titled "Market 2000" that assorted Nasdaq practices are prohibited on the New York and American exchanges but are still outside the domain of the securities laws as they are currently written and interpreted.

Our friend Sam Simon, the specialist who made out like a bandit with Widget, shakes his head in disgust when talking about Nasdaq market makers. Some of his peers believe that the market makers have been presented with a gilt-edged license to print money at the expense of a fair market for the average investor. One specialist of my acquaintance—not Sam Simon—has a long collection of stories about Nasdaq market makers and says bluntly, "Those people are thieves. They should shut down the over-the-counter market and hang those market makers."

The veteran Wall Street watcher Floyd Norris wrote in his "Market Watch" column in the Sunday *New York Times* in early 1994, "When you hire a broker to be your agent, should you expect that broker to look out for your best interests, or to ignore them in an effort to increase his own profits? Unfortunately, all too often, the brokers who make markets in Nasdaq stocks figure that customers are there to be exploited rather than served."

For their part, the market makers reel off their own list of episodes in which the specialists on the New York and American exchanges have cooked their books and trading for their own benefit.

The irony here is that the collective record of specialists, and even that of the market makers, is relatively clean. Even in the red-hot 1980s, when so many Wall Street chiefs were whisked off to jail for assorted mishaps, these men and women came through with a nearly unblemished record. Let's give them credit for that. Evidently, they aren't called specialists for nothing.

Front-Running

A market maker on the OTC market—the brokers' broker for Nasdaq—has a license to open a bank. What about the retail broker—*your* broker, the one who passes your order along to the market maker? Well, this upstanding citizen of Wall Street is not exactly waiting in line for a handout either. He can play his own version of the market maker's game explained in the preceding chapter.

Say an investor directs her broker to buy DNA Inc. at $10, as currently quoted on the Nasdaq exchange. A couple of hours later she receives confirmation for shares bought at $10¼ and naively assumes that the stock rose that quarter of a point in the few minutes between the placing of her order and its execution. Indeed, the price rose, but the reason for this would outrage this naive soul. The stock rose because the broker executed the trade for DNA shares at $10 for *his own account,* then sold those shares to *her account* for $10¼. What if the stock had slipped slightly below $10 around the time of this investor's order to buy? The broker could have ignored her order, bought the shares for himself at $9⅞, then fullfilled her order at $10.

This is the most flagrant form of front-running yet invented, and it happens all the time on the Nasdaq exchange. It happens hundreds of times every day, and according to Nasdaq rules, it's perfectly legal. In fact, the variations on this chicanery are almost endless, and they all result from manipulating the age-old "bid-and-asked" procedure for trading OTC stocks. The scenario with DNA Inc. sketched above is a simplified version of what actually happens. Here's a more detailed illustration of how a broker can work the "bid" and the "asked" to his or her advantage.

The bid is the highest price the prospective buyer is willing to pay, and the asked is the lowest price acceptable to a prospective seller of the stock. The difference between the two numbers is the "spread," and this is what the broker should announce as the quotation on any stock. The bigger the spread, the better for the broker.

Let's say the broker receives an order from "Gloria," one of his trusted clients, to buy 5,000 shares of ICC Technologies. That's good news for the broker, because ICC, which markets environmentally beneficial systems for climate control and energy efficiency that are used mainly in commercial buildings, was the subject of an item I wrote in *Business Week*'s "Inside Wall Street" that very day.

That column created a fair amount of activity in ICC. The bid on the stock was between \$3¾ and \$4. The asked quote was \$4½ to \$5.

The broker executed the order for Gloria at the upper end of the asked price range, very likely all the way up to \$5, explaining to his client that this was the best price he could obtain for her at the time.

But in truth the broker was able to buy shares at the *lower* end of the asked price, \$4½. However, he bought them at this favorable price for his own or his company's account or perhaps for a dummy account set up for just such situations. Then he sold the same shares to his own client for a profit. The broker made a commission off the deal *plus* a little trading income on the side. This is perfectly legal—not perfectly fair but perfectly legal.

Gloria's mistake lay in her failure to place a "limit order" on the stock. *Especially* when one is buying on the Nasdaq exchange, limit orders are a very good idea. But even with a limit order, the broker may be able to stall until the spread on the stock slips below the specified price on the limit order and then play that spread and execute the transaction as was described above, to his own benefit mainly.

Say Gloria had placed a limit order of \$4 on ICC Inc. Her broker could simply have informed her after a few hours that the market had left her behind on this stock. In other words, he wouldn't be able to execute the order at \$4. Would Gloria go as high as … \$4¾? Maybe he could get it at \$4½; he'd try, but the stock was moving, he might have to go to \$4¾. Gloria gives her reluctant approval.

Yes, this kind of manipulation happens. The real shame here is that everyone on Wall Street knows that it happens. As was noted above, the Securities and Exchange Commission also knows that it happens. The SEC has officially urged the Nasdaq market, which is theoretically a regulatory body as well as a licensing body, to adopt the rules against front-running used in the New York and American exchanges. On those exchanges, if a stock trades below the customer's limit order, the transaction must be executed. On those exchanges the transaction must be executed at the lowest available asking price.

The SEC urged Nasdaq to "adhere to certain minimum standards of fair treatment of customers." Richard Ketchum, Nasdaq's Executive Vice President, replied that his market will consider barring flagrant front-running practices. But why are we waiting for Nasdaq to regulate Nasdaq? Why doesn't the SEC simply dictate these basic changes, as it has the authority—and the obligation, one might argue—to do?

Of late, government regulators appear to have awakened to part of what is going on at Nasdaq. On October 17, 1994, the U.S. Justice Department said that it was investigating alleged price-fixing on the Nasdaq stock market, which some people have described as something like a free-for-all market, where almost anything goes. Junius Peake, a former vice chairman of Nasdaq and now a professor at the University of Northern Colorado, had this to say about the Nasdaq stock market when interviewed about it by *The Wall Street Journal* on October 18, 1994: "The Nasdaq stock market is kind of like a Middle Eastern bazaar, with people all trying to call you into their stall and sell you the same merchandise."

The ex-Nasdaq official, who would of course know the inside goings-on in the Nasdaq, says the government's decision to investigate should "expose the longstanding problems, and it may force some changes." The Justice Department has acknowledged that it was investigating charges in certain investor lawsuits and in two academic studies that allege that market makers on the Nasdaq system collude to rig up prices. The department's lawyers are probing the likelihood of what they politely term as "anticompetitive practices."

Predictably, the Nasdaq officials have denied vigorously that the market makers are committing any wrongdoing. Retorted Nasdaq's Ketchum: "This market is stringently overseen by the SEC and the National Association of Securities Dealers (Nasdaq). We are confident that the Justice Department review will show that market making in the Nasdaq stock market is highly competitive, and that the litigation is unfounded."

The Justice Department probe was provoked by some twenty-four lawsuits filed by some investors against securities firms that make markets on the Nasdaq, including some of the major investment houses on the Street. Many of the allegations involve what I have described earlier in this chapter. The lawsuits allege that market makers connive to maintain wide bid-and-ask spreads, which, as I have explained, represent the kind of profits that the market makers pile up.

The government investigation was partly ignited by two academic studies written by William G. Christie, a professor at Vanderbilt University, and Paul H. Schultz, assistant professor at Ohio State University. The study specifically charged that market makers have traditionally kept spreads at 25 cents a share wider, in contrast to narrower spreads of one-eighth of a point, or 12.5 cents a share, for most stocks listed on the Big Board and the American Stock Exchange. The Nasdaq employs many dealers to make markets in individual stocks, as opposed to one specialist for each stock in the stock exchanges. A second study done by the two professors concludes that some Nasdaq dealers narrowed their spreads to one-eighth of a point on May 27, 1994, the day after the first study was published. Lawsuits were filed against securities firms making markets in the Nasdaq right after the publication of the studies.

The studies appear to have accomplished part of their objectives. Says Professor Schultz: "It seems we dropped a match on some gasoline.... There are a lot of people out there upset with Nasdaq for various reasons, and this apparently galvanized them." One lawyer representing investors who have filed one of the lawsuits said the narrowing of the spread after the study was made public was the "most damning piece of evidence" indicating price-fixing on the Nasdaq system.

What's the response of the market makers? They deny any wrongdoing, as Richard Ketchum of the Nasdaq has said. Here's what one of the biggest market makers, E. E. "Buzzy" Geduld, President of Herzog, Heine, Geduld, Inc., a large New York trading firm, had to say when confronted by the *Journal* about the inquiry: "There's no conspiracy. An enormous amount of trades get done everyday in between the spread, and I think that speaks for itself." Ketchum explained that the quotes are simply the bid and offer that the market maker puts out, asserting that "trades occur, at narrower intervals all the time."

Maybe so—if the market maker chooses to do so. But how often does he pick up the phone and execute trades at the narrower spreads? Not often enough, according to many investors, and not always, that's for sure. For as long as it's legal for him to do what he pleases with formulating the spreads, the market maker will widen spreads as much as the market will bear.

One other practice that results in investors not getting a good price for shares that they buy has to do with the practice called "paying for order flow." That means, simply put, that a Nasdaq maker pays a brokerage house a certain fee for the right to execute orders for this brokerage firm's customers. This practice results in investors not always getting the most competititve price on stocks that they buy. It is nothing more than a monopoly-hold that the market makers have established on the customers of a brokerage firm. That fee that market makers pay to the brokerage firm for such exclusive rights has to come from somewhere. And it certainly will have to come from a bigger profit in the stock transactions that the market makers execute for that brokerage firms' customers.

This particular practice is also the subject of recent law-suits that have been filed against some Nasdaq market mak-ers. "At least one class-action lawsuit has been filed alleging that retail investors have received a less-than-best price on the Nasdaq market because of 'payment for order flow,'" says Harold Bradley, head trader for Twentieth Century Mutual Funds.

The smoke coming from the enclave of Nasdaq market makers has finally caught the attention of government authorities and regulators. Will they be able to spot the fire and put it out? Time will tell....

I do not want to leave the impression that front-running is restricted to operators on the Nasdaq exchange. Not at all. It is a broad category of malfeasance, and it can happen any-time, anyplace, as a young securities analyst I shall call "Larry Norton" found out the hard way.

Norton was a young analyst at a regional securities firm which also used to have a big presence in New York. Like most new people on any job, Larry was fiercely anxious to make a big impression on his employers. What better way to do this in the financial world than to discover the one big play that can make a name forever?

Larry's strength happened to be in the forestry and paper industry. His academic background was really in engi-neering. But because of his innate fascination with anything to do with forestry, Larry got to know everything about forests, trees, pulp, paper, and every stage in between. And of course his sheepskin in and of itself impressed many of the top people at his firm. When Larry wrote research papers on the companies assigned to him in that industry, his bosses, as well as Larry, were satisfied that they were on a par with, perhaps even more reliable than, the work of his peers at top-drawer New York houses such as Goldman, Sachs and Morgan Stanley.

Early one Monday morning in May 1986 a tiny story on page 4 of *The Wall Street Journal* received more than Larry's normal attention. The government had decided to acquire large tracts of property in California that were endowed with stands of gigantic redwood trees. The plan was to incorporate this acreage into a national park. Environmentalists were all for the idea, but their concerns were far from Larry's at that time. He was a securities analyst. He related *everything* to corporations and their stocks. (And he still does, in a different capacity. Larry is now an investment banker on his own.)

On this morning he instantly related this inconspicuous piece of news about the redwoods to one company— Louisiana-Pacific—which he knew owned the largest collection of properties in that region of California.

This is my key to stardom! Larry thought. This is my stock of destiny. Louisiana-Pacific. Larry was proud that he made the immediate connection between that bit of news on page 4 and a terrific investment opportunity. He had high hopes that the hundred grand his parents had plunked down for his diploma was going to pay off faster than they or he had imagined.

Norton rushed into his boss's office and blurted out, "I'm going to write a major report on Louisiana-Pacific. It involves a recent government decree on redwoods."

"Hold on, Larry," "Raines Merritt"—a pseudonym—said. "Don't rush into anything until you explain to us just what the hell you're talking about."

Larry was only too willing to explain: "The government has decreed that it will protect the redwood trees in California. Yesterday the Department of Natural Resources announced it would spend $1 billion to buy as much property in California's redwood forest region as possible and incorporate it in a national park."

"So what, Norton?" Raines interrupted. "Tree lovers and environmentalists are rejoicing, and loggers and developers are organizing demonstrations and raising hell." Merritt was an impatient elder statesman with this staid old firm, and like a lot of the top-producing stockbrokers who move up the corporate ladder in the securities industry (and all other industries too), he enjoyed jerking the chains of young employees. He started stacking up the papers on his desk as he glanced over at his co-managing partner, a man I will camouflage with the name "Randolf Warren."

Larry Norton persisted. "Mr. Merritt, this is one mother of a bonanza for L-P. If the company disposes of its redwoods, it could get at least $350,000 per acre. That works out to about $10 a share, and it will be *tax-free* because it is the federal government buying the property."

By then Merritt had stopped stacking his papers and seemed to be listening. Norton hurried forward.

"With its current cash flow of $3 a share, the stock is worth twice what it's trading for today."

"What is that, Larry?"

"Ten dollars."

Merritt stood up as a way of ending the discussion. He offered no final opinion on the idea. Neither did Randolf Warren, who packed up his own stuff. If anything, Warren showed even less interest in this idea than Merritt had.

"Talk to the company and check them out on your conclusions," Merritt concluded. "We want to be sure about this. You could be wrong in your optimistic conclusions, you know."

"I don't have to check much of anything, Mr. Merritt," Larry said with enough force to surprise even himself. "With all due respect, sir, I think I know what the score is here, and if you don't object, I should really go ahead and write up a strong buy recommendation on L-P."

"No, no, Larry. Hold off. Please check with the company, okay?" Merritt said.

Then Warren chimed in: "Let's put more thought into this. We should wait until we do the due diligence on this. And call the forestry division or natural resources or whatever and double-check on that decree. Just to confirm."

"Due diligence" is Wall Street jargon for spadework: extensive research and valuation. Norton respected Warren more than he respected Merritt, and so he was disappointed that Warren had failed to take up the cudgels for him on this one. He also couldn't figure out why neither man had expressed much interest in what looked like a fairly easy opportunity now that he had pointed it out. But young and fresh as he was, Larry wasn't totally without Street smarts. The thought crept into his mind that maybe, just maybe, Merritt and Warren were front-running Louisiana-Pacific at that very moment, one-upping their clients and their analyst as well.

But Larry preferred to think better of his bosses. For the rest of the day he worked on other stocks. The tape on L-P was fairly quiet. The following day Larry learned from a trader that his two bosses and a handful of other executives had all put in orders for call options on L-P. For a small premium they could purchase the stock anytime in the next two months for $10. Disappointed but not shocked, Norton said nothing. The following day L-P was finally making the move upward that Larry had anticipated all along. The stock was up to $12. Merritt called in his young analyst and said he'd been thinking about their previous discussion; maybe Larry had indeed stumbled across something valuable.

"Did you do some more work on Louisiana-Pacific?"

Larry said he had and went off to write his very bullish— and now very late—report.

Two weeks later Louisiana-Pacific had risen 100 percent, to $20 for just the reasons Larry had been the very first to understand. He figured his bosses had made a combined $2 million on those $10 call options on the stock—the most egregious kind of unethical front-running scheme. For his part in the party Larry was tossed a modest bonus by

Raines Merritt, Randolf Warren, and the other conspirators, and he even became some kind of star at the firm.

The Honest Stockbroker

As Merriweather and Warren prove, once a stockbroker, always a stockbroker, no matter how high one may rise in the company. It's no wonder that a broker named Michael Bertan of Advest Group Inc. received a fair amount of notoriety in the Spring of 1994 when he advertised himself in the *New York Press*, a local weekly publication, as the "Honest Stockbroker." Bertan attracted phone calls from some serious investors and some irritated rival stockbrokers as well. *The Wall Street Journal* ran a brief story on this uncommon advertisement featuring his bizarre claim. There was some question whether the New York Stock Exchange, which regulates the advertisements of member firms such as Advest Group, would frown on this particular ad, even though it did not mention Advest Group by name. (The ad did not even mention Michael Bertan's name. It simply listed a phone number.)

The source of the discomfort on the Street caused by Bertan's advertised claim to be an honest stockbroker is obvious. Such a claim implicitly charges a lot of other brokers with dishonesty, and that subject is one that the different stock exchanges and their member firms would just as soon ignore. As a rule, they don't talk about the subject, just as lawyers don't talk about it. The powers that be in both professions feel that nothing can be gained from even bringing up the subject of honesty, and they may be correct to fear guilt by association, especially if there's not much they're either willing or able to do about dishonesty in their profession. Certainly the Nasdaq market is better off distancing itself from the issue.

Still, the issue of honesty is impossible to avoid altogether as various charges and investgations keep cropping up. In 1993 the Prudential Securities fraud was a disaster for that brokerage house and an embarrassment for Wall Street in general. Stories about brokers and bosses in other firms fleecing naive and often elderly customers while soothing their concerns with scripted phrases like "just relax" are bound to create a ripple effect of disfavor for the entire industry, especially in Congress.

In 1994 the SEC announced much closer scrutiny of the 50,000 licensed stockbrokers in the United States. The obvious target of any such investigation will be the awesomely productive brokers who can legitimately be suspected of "churning" commissions from inattentive or unsuspecting clients.

But the truth is that nothing significant will change until the means of paying stockbrokers changes. As long as they work on commission, they will behave that way. The analogy with sharks may be a cliché by now, but it's still true: Both species have to keep on the move or they die.

Given the fact that stockbrokers are by definition sales-people motivated by the desire not just to make a living but to cash in big just as all their friends and associates on the Street are doing, and given all the temptations and oppor-tunities to take advantage of their knowledge of the myste-rious and arcane world of high (and low) finance, it's sur-prising that many brokers and specialists and, yes, even Nasdaq market makers are honest professionals who really are working on behalf of their clients.

But don't ask me whether "many" is also "most." That might be pushing it.

William McLucas, chief enforcement officer for the SEC, told *The Wall Street Journal* that he intends to focus his inquiries on stockbrokers who are "unscrupulous, unsophis-ticated—or both."

That distinction between unscrupulous and merely unso-phisticated stockbrokers is not an idle one by any means. For the serious investor who's wise to the ways of front-running and churning, the larger concern may be finding a stock-broker who's truly on the inside when it comes to valuable information. Some brokers are just simpletons who aren't even capable of finding the name of a stock in the newspa-per listings. These hapless souls are pretty easy to spot and therefore avoid. Tougher to identify are the bright people on the Street who for one reason or another just aren't in the know. For the serious investor these well-meaning but unconnected stockbrokers are more dangerous than the fools, because an investor can be dealing with one and not know it. Your portfolio can even be performing decently with such a broker, especially if the bulls are running, but you will never be in line for the big score.

If anything in this book is clear by now, I hope it's that connections are everything on Wall Street. "Inside information"—whether of the legal or the illegal variety—is just another way of saying "inside connections." This is true not only for arbitrageurs like Max Rosenthal and bagmen like Jack Flaherty; it's also true for basic stockbrokers and their clients. The brokers who hit the big time (and carry their favored clients along with them) are those who attach themselves to their firms' top analysts and/or investment bankers. A stockbroker who can do no better than rely on the company's research reports is probably going to have a hard time keeping his or her head above water. He or she is definitely not going to be able to deliver to his or her best clients the deals that will *keep* those clients or attract more of their money.

In the earlier chapter that focused on securities analysts, we weren't talking about Vinnie DeVito's *published* reports on Pharmco Group or Tony Conti's *published* reports on Union Carbide. Such reports aren't just old news; they're ancient history one day after they're published. Two days, max. Yes, the official pronouncements of the star analysts are good for a quick spike (or dip) in the market for that stock, as I have explained, but the retail broker can't wait for the news to spread to take advantage of that spike. The broker and his or her clients have to move *before* the spike, by definition. To move with the spike is to *miss* the spike, or the best part of it.

A broker on the way up has to know about that report early, right along with the analyst's favored clients and associates, the brokerage firm's top brass and *their* favored clients and associates, and the top management of the company in question and *their* favored associates. Many of these individuals will have the inside track on a prime analyst's long-awaited report. This is a given. Unless a broker can get on board this bandwagon, he or she will be stuck with yesterday's plain vanilla information. This apprentice might as well quit the business unless he or she is content to chow down in the company cafeteria alongside the backroom people while his or her peers and better-connected contemporaries dine at "21."

Now, this is *not* to say that an investor should obtain illegal inside information. I'm advocating that you find the best, most well-connected stockbroker you can. You will not ask or know where the broker gets his or her information from, and you will not care. You just want a broker who produces results, who is connected. Without this inside position, even the best workers on the Street must fly blind.

Recall the story about Mona Capital and its analyst's bullish, stubborn, and ill-fated call on Knickerbocker. Mona acknowledged that this analyst was among the finest she had ever encountered on the Street. He was dedicated to the point of being "religious" about his work. But in that one instance he was working with just the *official* facts and figures and PR statements, while the market situation was responding to the *real* facts of the matter. Mona hated to fire this man, but she had to because he almost sank her company. She had to demand perfection. You should demand the same from your broker. Otherwise, you stand to lose your fortune and your future.

Investment bankers and corporate finance people who work on underwritings and other financing deals can be a rich source of business for the stockbroker. These people are not automatically out of the broker's league. The more resourceful stockbroker works and wangles to get in on the underwriting side of the business. He or she scouts for companies that need to raise capital. If he or she finds one, the broker puts this company into discussions with a trusted investment banker. A fat commission waits for any broker who brings in an underwriting client. And of course, the broker is perfectly positioned to take advantage of the initial offering of any stock in the deal, a subject we'll investigate in depth. This kind of inside underwriting deal is easy to set up in a small firm in which the underwriters, analysts, and brokers mix it up daily. There are never any "Chinese walls" in these firms, to separate underwriters from analysts and brokers.

One way or another, a stockbroker just has to get "inside." It's awfully cold outside. The average broker in a big Wall Street house is the most dispensable professional in the entire hierarchy. That's the truth. These brokers get pushed around rudely if they fail to meet the performance targets the company has established for them. A young, diligent, ambitious backroom employee eating a tuna on rye in the cafeteria may get more respect than does this nonplayer.

I know the details of an appropriate story that happens to have a happy ending. When veteran stockbroker Bob Berlin worked for Bear Stearns & Co. in the 1980s, on several different occasions he was literally thrown out of his office whenever his prorated monthly performance slipped below the targeted annual total of $500,000 in sales. Somebody from administration would come around and say, "Sorry, Bob, you have to vacate this office because so and so has the hot hand and gets an office." Bob would then move his desk along with his secretary and her desk, to a cramped area in a hallway somewhere.

While the top personnel at Bear Stearns were pulling down many millions each ($20 million each in 1993), Berlin put up with this humiliation for five years until early 1994, when he managed to pull ahead and join Bear Stearns's "top producers" in the million-dollar club. This gave him an opportunity to get back at what he describes as "those cold and calculating top honchos" at Bear Stearns. His newfound brokering talent caught the attention of recruiters for PaineWebber, the firm that's obsessed with becoming the next, or another, Merrill Lynch. PaineWebber offered the oft-slighted Bob Berlin a $500,000 fee just for signing with the firm, plus an annual basic salary 50 percent higher than that he was guaranteed at Bear Stearns. The average basic annual salary of brokers at most firms was between $75,000 and $150,000. But it is in commissions that brokers make up for the relatively low salaries.

Bob waited until the Friday when he was leaving—his last day on the job—to tell those "top honchos" at Bear Stearns that he was out of there. This type of last-moment notice is typical practice in the business. Why? Advance notice can be hazardous to your financial health. Let Bob explain as he flees toward the bank of elevators in the building on Park Avenue and 45th Street on his final Friday afternoon: "They grab your books and freeze your accounts so you can't take them with you. Then they call up your clients and ask them to stay with the firm. It's like a war, unfortunately. I loved working with some of the people at Bear Stearns, but I had to protect my backside. Otherwise they shoot you down like a dog."

By relating Bob's story I certainly don't intend to single out Bear Stearns as a bad company on the Street for a broker to work for. This kind of thing happens up and down the Street—and on the side streets too, and out in Boston and Houston and Denver and L A. It's the environment everywhere. (Even outside of Wall Street. Recall Larry Norton and the fast one pulled on him by his bosses. Larry's conclusion was understandable, if sad: "Next time I'll know what to do. To hell with everyone else. I watch out for number one from now on.")

Stockbrokering has evolved into a very demanding, nerve-racking, dicey job. It's a jungle out there, as they say. Intelligence helps, but the gift of gab, raw guts, cunning, a manipulative mind, and arrogance come in just as handy, maybe more so. (The same holds true for just about every job on the Street.)

Just five years ago there were about half a million stock-brokers in this country. Today, there is one-tenth that number. What happened? First, the recession forced many of the brokerage houses to let people go. Second, there was a meteoric rise of the discount brokers and mutual funds.

Discount brokers such as the ubiquitous Charles Schwab have taken about 70 percent of the business that small individual investors used to direct at traditional brokers. When Schwab teams up with the mutual fund industry, the traditional brokerage houses find themselves between a rock and a hard place. Schwab alone has custody of $50 billion in assets.

So far, at least, the mutual funds have proved to be safe havens for money, yielding better returns than do competing vehicles, certainly better than certificates of deposit and passbooks. In any event, all this cut-rate competition for the investing dollar has played havoc with the full-service brokerage houses and their brokers. The mediocre performers are cut loose and wash up on the beach daily. Only the seasoned and savvy, only the brokers who somehow wangle their way onto the inside track, still thrive. That's how Bob Berlin finally got out of the doghouse at Bear Stearns—and then out of Bear Stearns entirely.

All in all, has this shift away from full-service brokerage been beneficial? In the case of the big institutional investors it's a moot question. Their assets give them so much clout with the full-service firms, they can negotiate discounted fees and keep the full service too. Also, the cushy, even incestuous relationship between those investors and Wall

Street partners guarantees that everyone will be taken care of. But for the average small investor I don't think the change has been good. Investors who have gone with the discount brokers are getting exactly what they pay for: next to nothing. In most cases the discounters live up to their name, offering low-cost, no-frills, no-nonsense service. They take orders and execute trades, period (although Schwab is now including certain value-added services, such as a selection of mutual funds to invest in, at no cost). Basically, the average investor with a discount brokerage is on his or her own, and that's not a good place to be in the financial world.

Meanwhile, over at the full-service houses, the field has been left in the hands of those "seasoned and savvy" brokers who survived the big shakeout of the past five years. The question becomes, Are they savvy in that they know the markets and steer their clients into the best opportunities, or are they savvy in that they know how to manipulate their clients' trading to their own benefit (as in, for example, the various front-running schemes so common on the Nasdaq exchange)?

It depends, and it therefore behooves an investor who has stayed with a full-service house to determine which category his or her broker fits into. But it can be safely said that most brokers have too many clients and will naturally work the hardest for the biggest ones. The last person on almost any broker's list will be the small investor whose trading is picayune compared with the volumes generated by institutional investors.

There you have it. The terrain is difficult for investors with or without the help of brokers. The shakeout in the brokerage industry has caused thousands of brokers to leave the industry. That's both good and bad. The upside is that the drop in the number of brokers has, by simple math, also reduced mediocrity in the business and the number of rotten apples. But there is no guarantee that their replacements will be any better. When the next boom cycle comes around, the current vacuum might well be filled by another batch of incompetents.

Real Inside Information

Generally speaking, a stockbroker, no matter how excellent, remains a notch or two below the highest echelons of the Wall Street pecking order. The best stockbrokers move on to become *former* stockbrokers, but not always. The Canadian turned Californian Douglas A. Campbell is a case in point. Armed with a B.A. from McGill University, an MBA from Harvard, and a Ph.D. in economics from Columbia, he has been in the business for more than thirty-five years and now runs his own brokerage firm, D. A. Campbell Co., in Los Angeles. In fact, Campbell is one of those uncommon individuals who started out in brokering (Greenshields & Co. in Montreal), moved into analysis (Kidder Peabody & Co. in New York), but then returned to retail salesmanship.

In the eyes of the financial press Campbell does not have the star power of, say, Peter Lynch and the legendary John

Templeton, but he's on the level of those stars and their peers in the only way that really counts: He has their ear and their respect. Campbell also has the reputation of being a straight shooter and an honest man. In his main field of expertise—Mexico, where he lived for several years, and Latin America—his knowledge and insight are all he needs to lap the field. He demonstrates that a tenacious stockbroker who does his or her own hard and honest research in a focused area can dig up "real" inside information that makes him or her an indispensable investment ally of the best investors and traders in the business. The man with the shock of thick white hair and the perennial tan almost gives a good name to the phrase "inside information."

Campbell pays little attention to U.S. stocks. Instead, he savors looking for undervalued shares in foreign markets, mainly in our neighbors to the south. The story of his incredible successes with Telefonos de Mexico is a prime case in point. It's also a lesson in how big players on the Street such as Templeton, Lynch, and Campbell share the wealth among themselves—but not with inside information in this case.

Telefonos de Mexico (TelMex) was formed when a group of Mexican businesspersons acquired the local assets and operations of Sweden's L. M. Ericsson and America's International Telephone and Telegraph Co. in 1947. By 1958 TelMex had become Mexico's telecommunications monopoly, and in 1972 the government took over control of the company by buying 51 percent of the stock. In the 1980s Campbell began acquiring shares for himself and his clients at a time when the stock was virtually unknown in this country. But Campbell understood that TelMex was just beginning to evolve from a bureaucratic fossil providing basic domestic telephone services with antiquated equipment into a provider of international telecommunications services using modern digital technology. The number of subscribers in Mexico was on the rise; new products and services were under way.

In 1986 he picked up the phone and called Peter Lynch in New York, who was flying about as high as it's possible to fly with the giant Fidelity Magellan Fund.

You might think that a superstar like Lynch would have little interest in or need of a stockbroker's advice, but he would certainly take a call from a man of Campbell's reputation. In fact, Lynch had an "open line" in the early-morning hours for select brokers and analysts. There was one catch: Each suitor had one minute to make his or her pitch.

"It was like name, rank, and serial number," Campbell enjoyed joking later.

At four-thirty in the morning, West Coast time, Campbell was ready with his spiel to the formidable Peter Lynch: "Telefonos de Mexico, P-E of 3, selling at only a third of book value, 50 percent of earnings in U.S. dollars from foreign billings, now selling at 12 cents a share. I could get you a lot of these tremendously undervalued shares, Peter."

To Campbell's surprise, Lynch replied that he already knew about TelMex and had just bought some of its American depositary receipts (ADRs), each representing twenty shares. TelMex has two kinds of ADRs trading in the United States. One of them is equal to one underlying TelMex share and trades on the Nasdaq market with the symbol TFONY. The other is equal to twenty TelMex shares and trades on the Big Board with the symbol TMX.

"Peter," Campbell implored instantly, "instead of buying the ADRs, you should buy the actual shares directly in Mexico, which come out much cheaper. It's the way to accumulate a lot more. This will be the stock of the century."

Lynch was silent for a moment. Then he said, "Okay, Doug, we'll buy 5 million shares at 12 cents to start." Campbell was ecstatic of course. After all, he was a stockbroker—a salesperson—and this was a nice commission.

A week before Campbell called Lynch he had called John Templeton, a close friend who had handled Campbell's investments many years before, when the Canadian had first settled in the United States. The main reason for the call was that a friend of Campbell's, Jerry Murphy, president of Erly Industries Inc., wanted his help in buying back shares of his company. The largest shareholder of Erly? John Templeton. Erly stock was trading at $7 a share. Campbell brokered the deal for 500,000 shares at $10 apiece.

Campbell then switched subjects with his friend Templeton, urging him to take a look at TelMex. Again the stockbroker was surprised to learn that Templeton, like Lynch, already knew about TelMex and owned a block of shares for the Templeton Fund. Campbell pressed him to buy more shares, reminding him that this was his favorite stock *in the world.* To Campbell's delight, Templeton ponied up for an additional 8 million shares.

Then came the shocker. Templeton, the buyer in this deal, had a scoop for Campbell about TelMex. Templeton revealed that he knew how to acquire the shares for 4 cents, not 12!

Campbell was nonplussed. TelMex was *his* company. He knew it cold. He knew Mexico cold. Four cents would be the "private placement" to beat all private placements. How could it be? Templeton explained that TelMex had devised a plan to raise extra cash by requiring each new subscriber to buy a share for 4 cents. In order to convince subscribers to hold on to these shares, TelMex would promise to pay a cash and stock dividend two years after the purchase. What's more, Templeton revealed, he knew that practically all the subscribers just wanted the telephone service and didn't care to own stock. These people would sell their shares for 4 cents!

How did Templeton know about this plan? As a large TelMex investor, he had contacts in the company that were as good as Campbell's—better in this instance. One of the blessings of being a major shareholder is access to helpful "insidy" stuff.

Doug Campbell immediately realized the brilliance of the plan as outlined by Templeton, obtained the names of TelMex subscribers, enlisted the aid of local Mexican brokers, and eventually succeeded in buying more than 8 million shares for Templeton at a price of 4 to 6 cents a share. He also passed this windfall along to Peter Lynch.

Even after the Peter Lynch and John Templeton purchases through Douglas Campbell, TelMex stock was rela-

tively quiet. Nevertheless, Lynch kept adding shares to
Fidelity's stake. By the spring of the following year, 1987,
the stock had started its move, climbing smartly to 20 cents.
Three months later it hit 80 cents. By that time Campbell
sensed that the stock had started to get ahead of itself. He
called Lynch and suggested that he start cashing in the
humongous profits on his stake, which was now 55 million
shares. Lynch agreed and sold the shares at an average of 70
cents apiece. Successes like that with relatively obscure foreign stocks are one way in which Fidelity Magellan established itself as one of the flagships of mutual funds.

Templeton stayed in with his long-term strategy, which
has yielded tremendous returns over the years.

But the game in TelMex was not over by any means, and
Campbell knew it. He knew there would be another opportunity to get back into the stock and ride it all the way up
again, and this opportunity came sooner rather than later.
Within a couple of months of the Lynch sale, the stock had
dropped down to 18 cents. When it rallied back to 30 cents,
Campbell felt certain that the selling had dried up.

He was back on the phone to Peter Lynch again, and this
time he probably got more than the one minute of air time
allotted to the rank and file. The Fidelity Magellan miracle
man agreed again. Lynch purchased a second set of 55 million shares at 30 cents a share. When Peter Lynch quit
Magellan in 1992, the fund still had most of those shares.
By 1993 TelMex was trading for $5 on Nasdaq's Small Cap
OTC market—another gigantic profit for Magellan. By 1994
the stock had slipped to $3, but this was still a huge profit

for the early buyers. TelMex's ADR that trades on the Big Board also posted monster gains, climbing all the way to $65, as of late October 1994, which is a 450-fold increase since 1986.

John Templeton held on to most of his 8 million TelMex shares, which had cost him all of $32,000 in 1986. Counting stock and cash dividends, this stake reached a value of about $64 million when TelMex hit its high mark of $5.

Hordes of other investors have made money off TelMex, now the foreign stock of choice for many American investors. One cause for confidence in the stock is that more than 40 percent of the company's annual revenues are generated in the United States (by way of long-distance calls emanating from the United States). Another is that TelMex is now 100 percent publicly owned. The Mexican government began privatizing the company in 1991 and in 1994 sold all of its remaining interest to Southwestern Bell, France Telecom, and Grupo Carso. This trio now owns 51 percent of the voting stock.

As for Doug Campbell, the TelMex bonanza was hardly a flash in the pan. When D.A. Campbell Co. started in 1986, it posted annual gross earnings of $350,000. By 1993 that number had ballooned to $8.4 million. Campbell enjoys life at his Los Angeles mansion with the two-story fountain of hand-chiseled Mexican *roja-cantero* stone, but his chief passion is still studying that large pool of Latin American companies virtually unknown on Wall Street in order to find the next TelMex, and the next one, and the next one....

The Program to End All Programs

Douglas Campbell deals in real companies, real information, intrinsic worth. He's living proof that investing on the basis of spadework can yield dividends and more than dividends. On the opposite end of the spectrum from investors who deal in the fundamentals are those who specialize in "program trading," now so popular on the New York Stock Exchange, and in the "small-order execution system" (SOES) equivalent on the Nasdaq over-the-counter market. Campbell's efforts are an undoubted benefit to the markets and to the companies he finds and supports. These high-tech sleight-of-hand program trading schemes have little redeeming social or economic value whatsoever. These computer guerrillas give a whole new slant to the phrase "insider trading." Their market machinations are so far "inside" the computers, they never see the light of day at all.

The irony is that the intricate software programs that allow program and SOES trading were designed to *protect* unsophisticated small investors. That altruistic motivation stemmed from the market catastrophe of October 19, 1987, when the Dow Jones plunged 500 points. The crash came without warning, and the biggest losers were the small investors. Overwhelmed stockbrokers tried their best to take care of favored clients; phone calls from small investors went unanswered and unreturned. In effect, stockbrokers staged an unannounced and costly strike, and this unconscionable behavior aggravated the already devastating decline of the market. Without access to their brokers, small investors who wanted to bail out—or bargain hunt—were locked out, in effect. The following day they were outraged, and to the credit of all the major Wall Street markets, they took immediate steps to assure that such a lockout could not occur again.

The Big Board had put in place some years earlier a "direct-order trading" system that facilitated practically instant execution of orders electronically. Nasdaq, the organization that oversees the OTC market and tolerates the manipulations of market makers and brokers discussed in an earlier chapter, did the right thing this time and bolstered its own mechanism for rapid-execution trading—SOES.

Each innovation was designed to give any investor access to the markets at any time through his or her broker, and each does this. But each also has had an unintended consequence. The so-called program traders on the New York and American exchanges play the new computerized trading system for all it's worth. Massive orders to buy followed within seconds by massive orders to sell may be nothing more than "technical" transactions that take advantage of tiny price fluctuations, but they artificially influence the direction of stock prices. They would have to, since program trading runs to billions of dollars at any given time.

Program trading has long been a controversial element in the market, with the massive flow of money through these focused program-driven trades often being blamed for violent swings and moves in one direction or another. If the market is weak, this argument goes, the barrage of selling from the program traders fuels even more selling when other investors see that the program traders have hit the market. Big Board member firms that specialize in program trading, such as Morgan Stanley and Goldman, Sachs, reject such accusations. They contend that program trades add liquidity to the market and *follow* the market's chosen direction rather than *lead* it. As you can imagine, the arguments and rebuttals on both sides get highly technical.

To see how the equivalent system works on the OTC market, let's follow a day in the life of a man named Harvey, a retiree who plays the market avidly at a regional brokerage house in upstate New York. Harvey has one main investing strategy: exploit the SOES system. He arrives at the brokerage house at eight-thirty sharp on most mornings, an hour before the opening bell, and takes his seat next to Seymour, his favorite trader. In truth, Harvey is one of Seymour's favorite customers because, like most SOES fanatics, Harvey trades on average thousands of shares a day—a reasonably big source of commission income for Seymour and his company. Customers of lesser value would not be allowed to peer directly into the SOES system, much less execute trades from it. Some brokerage houses, particularly the larger ones, don't allow "bandits" on their trading floors, no matter how active they may be. Other companies welcome them. These firms want the commissions, and the bandit is present thanks to an informal agreement with the head trader.

As a team, Harvey the client and Seymour the broker-trader study the computer screen. For each Nasdaq stock, the latest bid and asked quotes are listed, along with the number of shares involved. Seymour has another terminal which relates important business news. Much of Harvey's trading is based on these developments. For example, if Harvey reads that a company is expected to issue a positive earnings statement, he will make a preopening bid for shares of that company. A stock can usually be counted on to jump a little immediately after a positive earning report or when there are profits above analysts' expectations. The first seller of the stock upon this eventuality? Harvey, of course, who is trading strictly in the shortest term possible. His buy order might be executed at exactly nine-thirty, and his sell order minutes later.

Now, recall the function of the Nasdaq market maker who was introduced in an earlier chapter. When orders come in to buy a stock, this market maker promptly widens the spread between the new bid (buy) price and the asked (sell) price. His or her official function is to maintain an orderly flow of trades, but as we have seen, the market maker also trades for his or her own benefit. Therefore, the market maker will raise the buy price in order to make this spread as wide as the market will bear, because the spread is a rough indication of the profit that would result from trading for his or her own account.

In the old days the market maker was out in front of all other investors timewise and way out in front of individual investors spread around the country. But with the advent of SOES, the market maker is just seconds, maybe even just milliseconds, ahead of Harvey and Seymour seated in front of their terminals. When this trading team in upstate New York sees that the market maker in New York City has widened the bid-asked spread, as expected, they react instantly, selling shares at the high end of the bid price and chalking up a nice profit.

The immediate impact of the bandit's quickie sale is to raise the asked price for that stock. The unintended net effect of the SOES system is to assure that the average investor buys stock at the highest price. The investor is victimized to the benefit of Harvey the investor and Seymour the trader.

In situations in which there aren't enough available shares to buy, an SOES trader can make an even bigger killing. The trader withholds selling shares until the market maker raises the bid price still higher, to the highest possible price, at which time the SOES trader, studying the situation in what amounts to "real time" on the computer screen, decides from the goodness of his or her heart to supply the market with the shares.

Harvey executes about 250 trades a day—several dozen every hour. At that rate, the SOES bandit puts up as high as $20,000 or as little as $5,000. For a transaction of that size the brokerage house charges Harvey about $8 per trade. In one day it makes about $2,000 from Harvey's transactions, with virtually no cost or risk to the house. And that number for brokerage fees gives us an indication of how much Harvey earns from his SOES trading. He's a shrewd investor. He's not paying these kinds of commissions for the fun of it. He estimates that his annual earning are in the area of $500,000.

Are Harvey and Seymour breaking the law? Yes and no. Some critics contend that this kind of SOES trading constitutes stock manipulation pure and simple, but no specific regulation prohibits this activity—yet. As we speak, the SEC is promulgating new rules in an attempt to curb abuses of the SOES system. One rule will cut back on the number of shares that can be executed in any one SOES trade (this would probably not affect Harvey). Another attempts to curb the shorting of stocks through SOES (that might affect a trader like Harvey). Time will tell how effective the rules are in reigning in the SOES bandits.

If Harvey's kind of SOES trading is stock manipulation, so is the much more organized and profitable program trading at the New York Stock Exchange. What's more, Harvey's trading, along with the SOES trading of other "small investors" in the OTC market, is a pittance compared with the action generated by program traders on the Big Board. The two trading systems are similar in principle and execution and identical in outcome.

The Money Machine

've suggested once or twice that extraordinarily well placed Wall Street operators—the Nasdaq market makers come to mind—have "a license to print money," but in doing so I was using that phrase somewhat loosely. Now I will use it literally. Wall Street really *does* have such a license. It's called the initial public offering (IPO). Who knows where the buck stops, but it *starts* right here. The IPO system is the money machine for the free enterprise system.

Common sense tells us that this authorized permission to get rich quick—this extraordinary cash cow known in Street parlance as the IPO—is rife with insider trading. The two go hand in hand—all the way to the august halls of Congress, as we shall see.

The fun begins when a small start-up company approaches one of the hundreds of underwriters on Wall Street. Underwriters also go by the more exalted title *invest-*

ment bankers. These gentlemen and gentlewomen are approached hundreds of times a year by unknown capital-starved enterprises. And vice versa. The investment banks are the heroes of this horde of emerging, credit-*unworthy* companies with little earnings and no track records to speak of. If these companies don't score on Wall Street, they'll probably have to shut down. But if they do attract an investment bank to their cause, they have a brand new lease on life, with a legitimate chance to join the big leagues or at least Triple A.

Without a doubt this opportunity to raise capital is a vital feature of free enterprise. If a worthwhile start-up raises the necessary capital in an IPO and goes on to become an upright citizen in corporate America, that's nice, but it's a strictly secondary consideration. The system is designed primarily to enrich and coddle insiders on Wall Street.

The investment bank is the backbone of the securities brokerage business. In many ways these huge commissions and underwriting fees support the whole operation. While generating these fees, the banks pretty much write their own ticket and establish their own guidelines. The parameters outlined by federal securities laws are fuzzy to begin with and are loaded with loopholes besides. It's safe to say that very few IPO offerings are aborted because of some federal regulation somewhere. The underwriters can and do finance almost any company they cotton to.

The basic rule states that the company and its investment bankers must reveal everything known about the company.

The risks have to be spelled out. If the IPO offering meets the letter of the law in this regard, it will almost certainly get final approval from the Securities and Exchange Commission, but there can be a lot of invisible ink hidden behind the letter of that law.

In 1982 New York's "John Smith & Co." underwrote a $10 million IPO for "NRT Co." "John Smith" was a modest-sized but aggressive and furiously active investment bank specializing in very small companies. NRT was presented as a budding high-tech firm servicing the real estate industry in northern California's Silicon Valley. Like all investment banks, John Smith had a stable of voracious clients, which in Smith's case included several of the biggest hedge fund operators on the Street. These clients were happy to take a flier on NRT, if for no other reason than that technology shares—almost all technology shares—were hot and approaching a boil at that time. The paperwork on the deal seemed to be in order. The John Smith number crunchers presented an impressive array of optimistic predictions, and the IPO shares were snapped up immediately.

The big day came, and "John Boxer," the jubilant president of John Smith, presented a check for $9 million to "Dr. White," the jubilant chairman and CEO of the newly capitalized NRT. (Just $9 million? Yes: the $10 million IPO offering minus the 10 percent fee for the bankers. Standard operating procedure for a deal this size.) Check in hand, Dr. White joked that now he could buy that mansion down in Beverly Hills he had had his eye on for quite some time. All the other NRT executives and New York bankers crowded into the conference room laughed with gusto. Cake and coffee and libations were served, and then everyone left in good spirits. Mr. Boxer and Dr. White shook hands one last time for a job well done on both sides.

And that was the last time anyone in that room laid eyes on the CEO of NRT. Chairman White disappeared, and so did the $9 million. When the John Smith bankers got wind of something amiss and flew to San Jose, headquarters of the company they thought they had just set up in business, they found an empty office building. The company had had only a six-month lease on the place. The furniture had been removed days before.

Apparently these bankers had not been quite diligent enough in their investigation of the bona fides of NRT. Apparently these consummate insiders had been somewhat more interested in generating that $1 million commission than in assuring at least a *reasonably* sound investment for their clients. And apparently shrewd investors like these clients of John Smith don't take such "mistakes" lightly. Within a year the firm was out of business.

The underwriting procedure is simple enough. The banker matches investors and their money with companies and their craving for that money. The investor hands over cold cash and receives in return a piece of paper. Whether this paper is a stock or a bond, the idea is the same: The investor is gambling on an idea in the hopes of getting a return on the investment. (Highly leveraged junk-bond financing comes down to the same thing. Michael Milken's genius, if we want to use that term in referring to a convicted felon, is that he understood that the psychology that leads investors to play the IPO game would also lead them to play the junk bond game. With the involuntary departure of Milken from the LBO scene, the focus on the Street has returned to where it was in the pre-Milken days: IPOs.) Indeed, Milken's notorious junk bonds are like a takeoff from the ubiquitous IPOs. Junk bonds are IOUs issued by cash-starved companies. IPOs are new shares issued by cash strapped young companies and are sold to investors. Milken exploited and took advantage of both the junk bond issuers and their buyers. The investment bankers or underwriters similarly exploit and take full advantage of IPO issuers and the IPO buyers. In both cases, the intermediaries invariably win.

The hazards for the investor are many and obvious. Maybe the enterprise is a total fraud, like NRT. Maybe it's not a total fraud but is a good deal more speculative than it purports to be. Maybe the investment bank did a good job evaluating the company and setting up the IPO, but maybe it didn't. Maybe a million things, given the fact that countless numbers of small businesses started up in the United States fold within twelve months. The same is true with IPOs. Never was the cautionary warning *caveat emptor* more important than in reference to investing in initial public offerings. But for insiders, what's the worry? They will proudly admit that there are any number of ways to skin an IPO offering, and most of these tricks require access to—what else?—inside information.

A key decision in underwriting an IPO is establishing the initial price of the stock. Because the underwriting fee is a percentage of the total capitalization sought—the number of shares multiplied by the initial asking price—the underwriter obviously has a vested interest in pricing the stock as high as the market will bear and issuing as many shares as that same market will bear. John Smith's $1 million fee for the $10 million capitalization of NRT is the industry standard. In addition, the investment bank will receive another 3 percent of the total capitalization to cover "unaccountable" expenses that may or may not be incurred by the underwriter. Total fee: 13 percent.

But that's just for beginners, literally. Next come the "warrants" that the team of underwriting bankers will negotiate for itself at the very outset. These warrants give the bankers the right to buy shares of the stock at somewhere between 10 and 25 percent of the initial offering price. The holders of the warrants retain this right for one year usually, and of course they do not have to exercise it. They can see how things are going first. Rest assured that the John Smith bankers discarded their NRT warrants into the circular file the day the money disappeared out in California. The same privilege for buying warrants will be extended to top brass of the company that is to be taken public, but at least they have to pay *something* for the warranted shares. However, they'll retain for themselves another block of shares for which they have paid nothing at all. After all, the public offering is their main opportunity for "cashing out" their stake in the company.

Because the underwriters' fee is a percentage of the total capitalization sought, it behooves the underwriters to convince themselves and the investment world that the company deserves the highest conceivable capitalization. Because their warrants become valuable in direct correlation with the price of the stock on the open market, it behooves the underwriters to convince the investment world that this company is the hottest thing going. Fortunes can be made in the first few days and weeks of an IPO. In fact, this is often the best time to make that fortune: The stock might shoot up and then flame out as quickly as a skyrocket.

Of course, the investment bankers have families and favored associates: investors, brokers, analysts, portfolio managers at the huge mutual funds and pension funds, and other worthwhile friends. They will alert those individuals to the impending windfall and invite them to buy a "private placement" of shares at prices lower than the initial offering price. This favoritism is a constant source of complaint about the IPO system.

One "average investor," Jeffrey Grossman, has gone public in *The Wall Street Journal* about his inability to get on the inside. He has contrasted his situation with that of one Gary Ackerman. Both men play the stock market, but they differ in two key respects. Grossman has been shut out of the lucrative IPO market, while Ackerman is often an invitee. Not coincidentally, Grossman charges, he's the city administrator of Westbrook, Maine, while Ackerman is a Democratic representative from New York.

Nor is the city administrator alone in decrying this kind

of politically advantageous favoritism. A good bit of attention has been focused lately on members of Congress who
are invited to the IPO trough before the rest of us. Speaker
of the House Tom Foley, Democrat of Washington, was
attacked by his opponent during the 1994 campaign for
cashing in on four IPO offerings worth about $100,000.

Here is an example of how this favoritism works in practice. These are actual figures from a typical episode. "Marty
Lane," an investment banker who specializes in taking small
health care companies public, calls the pseudonymous "Jonathan Meaders," a senior portfolio manager at a major mutual fund. The tantalizing offer: 50,000 shares of the forth-
coming XXX Corp. at $3 a share. In six or eight months
Marty's firm is taking XXX public at $10 share.

Many times the underwriter will offer choice clients many
more shares than the measly 50,000 Marty Lane offers
Jonathan Meaders. A hot IPO is an excellent way for a money
manager to make amends for any sour deals he or she may
have gotten a major client into. Dummy accounts may be set
up for this purpose. Dummy accounts are illegal. The SEC
assumes that if everything is kosher, buyers and sellers have
no reason to hide. A dummy account is considered almost
prima facie evidence of guilt. (On Wall Street, disclosure is
right next to godliness. Total disclosure can go a long way
toward establishing innocence. Many times, a corporate plan
or deal can be absurdly silly or dumb, but as long as everything is disclosed publicly, the SEC will not bother the parties
involved—at least not until an overt felony is committed.)

Of course, Jonathan Meaders has heard of this kind of private placement on an IPO before, but this is the first time that he has been offered the inside action. Nor is this surprising. The inside position on a hot IPO may be the crème de la crème of all the plays on the Street. You have to pay your dues in order to be invited. You might never be invited.

Jonathan Meaders hesitates. Is this trading on insider information? Of course it is. Then again, it's not inside information in the nasty sense of the term, because the company has not even been traded yet. It might never be traded. It might immediately go belly up, and Jonathan would be out his $150,000. So there's risk here. This deal as presented is probably not illegal, although a question could be raised about the "when and where" disclosure Lane gives Meaders.

After pondering the offer, Jonathan accepts: "I'm in! Definitely."

"Great. There's one more detail."

"What's that?"

"In return for this opportunity, you have to agree to buy another 100,000 shares at the initial offering price—the official price—when the time comes."

"Ten dollars?"

"Yeah, $10. And remember, Jonathan, if you get on board this time, you're on our private list for the next hot issue."

In a (very small) nutshell, this is how a hot offering is pulled out of the hat. This is how some of the Street's more creative underwriters are able to produce tantalizing, soon to be torrid IPOs out of thin air. The key to producing the hot IPO that makes those warrants so valuable is to pump up demand for the stock in what's called the aftermarket.

But this aftermarket begins immediately upon the issuance of the stock, and if sufficient demand has been generated, the IPO stock will zoom 50 or 100 percent above its initial price in a matter of hours. IPOs have soared 300 percent in one day, and such a spectacular opening-day performance can then fuel a continued run-up for weeks or several months.

In the case of XXX Corp. shares bought "inside" by Jonathan Meaders, the stock jumped from the initial price of $10 up to $35, then back down to $10 again and eventually all the way to $3. But by then Jonathan had cashed in all his shares at an average of $30. Therefore, on the 50,000 shares offered to him at $3, he made $1.35 million. On the 100,000 shares bought at $10, he made $2 million. Total: $3.35 million minus brokerage fees, which go to the *underwriter's* broker, of course.

The question comes up: Did Jonathan buy those shares and make this profit for himself, for the mutual fund he manages, or for both? The manager's behavior in these cases depends on his or her own ethics and the ethics and policies of the manager's employer. Front-running by mutual fund managers is illegal, and all funds have rules against such trading. But is it front-running to buy IPO shares (or any other shares, for that matter) for a personal portfolio *as well as* for the mutual fund? Does such a simultaneous purchase constitute front-running? After all, not every trade for a personal portfolio represents front-running. Who can say with certainty what the manager's motivation is? The line is thin between buying shares for a personal portfolio because the money manager honestly believes in the stock and buying personal shares (those 50,000 IPO shares at $3) because the manager knows that the shares will rise partly because he or she intends to buy many more shares later for the mutual fund (those 100,000 IPO shares at $10).

The money managers at one well-known mutual funds group, Fidelity Investments, do indeed trade for their own accounts, but other funds strictly prohibit the apparent conflict of interest caused by such personal trading. The large Invesco Funds Group, a large operator of mutual funds, was one of the first, if not the first, mutual fund to get involved in a case of personal trading by one of its managers. Invesco fired its star manager for his alleged failure to report some twenty trades for his own account. But over at Fidelity there are no such qualms. Some managers there reportedly rack up as many as 200 personal trades annually. The tradition of personal trading at Fidelity is closely associated with the career of the legendary Peter Lynch, whom we have already encountered in the story about Douglas Campbell and the phenomenal Telefonos de Mexico.

For thirteen years Lynch stewarded the multi-billion-dollar Fidelity Magellan Fund to the position of prominence it enjoys today among mutual funds. He retired in 1990. Acording to a Fidelity spokeswoman quoted in *The Wall Street Journal*, Lynch took out a personal loan in the 1970s to fund his personal trading. A Fidelity managing director was quoted in the *Journal* story as saying, "We're looking for people who trade for their own account. If managers have money at risk, they more fully appreciate what it's like for shareholders to have money at risk."

The arguments on both sides of this issue have merit. In any event, there's no doubt that fund managers whose employers allow them to carry personal portfolios are on the A list at Marty Lane's investment bank, and at all the others too.

However, Marty Lane isn't in a position to offer all the insiders shares at $3. There is a limit. The less preferred but still "inside" list is offered an allocation at the official offering price—$10 in the case of XXX Corp.

"But don't worry," Marty assures those investors. "This issue will be hot."

"How do I know?"

Because Marty and his fellow underwriters are veterans at rigging aftermarket demand. Forget what you might hear about the market being as unpredictable as the weather. An underwriter like Marty knows almost exactly how his stock will perform in the aftermarket, at least over the short run. After all, he's looking right at his lists of private placement clients, most-favored clients, and the second wave of somewhat-favored clients. He knows how many shares of XXX each of these investors is in for.

He knows the supply. He knows the demand. He knows the score. The word on the Street is out. The IPO for XXX is sold out. The moment the bell rings to begin trading on XXX, the second wave of $10 buyers is automatically in place. The initial price jumps within seconds. Investors who weren't on the inside are scrambling to get on board at the earliest possible time. The price jumps again and again and again, all the way through the roof. Demand is overwhelming supply, as it's supposed to do in an IPO. Where do the shares that are for sale come from? From the underwriters and the insiders, of course, who are selling—*judiciously*—into the rising tide of buying.

The underwriter wants the price of the stock to stay as high as possible for as long as possible, and so he or she has to control the supply. The underwriter may order his or her brokers to *refuse any sell orders* from the preferred and somewhat-preferred customers. Not everyone can cash in at the same time.

How do they get away with this? They just do—in the case of certain brokerage houses, time after time after time. The idea is to sustain the demand long enough to allow all the various insiders to buy stock on their warrants and then sell it for their phenomenal gain without overly depressing the stock.

In any event, once the insiders have cashed out, the stock is on its own. If it plummets back to where it should have been all along without all the manipulation and hype, if in the process of flaming out it burns the hapless noninsiders commonly known as the public, well, that's unfortunate, but that's the way the game is played.

Churn 'em and burn 'em. That's the lingo.

We have already met Tom Moore of Moore & Co. He was the young manager for the Amherst Fund who was offered and declined a $50,000 cash bribe by an executive of a large industrial company. At a younger age still, while a rookie broker at a small securities firm, Tom Moore had received another baptism under fire, this one in the highly charged world of IPOs.

The story starts in Harry's Bar on Hanover Square near Wall Street. One Friday evening at Harry's another broker of Moore's acquaintance regaled his junior with a series of glamorous get-rich-quick tales. Young and old, brokers love to exchange stories about their favorite windfalls of the past and perhaps embellish the facts in the process. No harm done. Moore had been involved in a number of such inevitably alcoholic conversations. But this time the broker I'll call "Ron Smart" went one step further and invited Moore in on the next big killing on the Street. Ron Smart is not his real name, of course, but it is his real nickname on the Street, whether he knows it or not, because he managed to lose $100,000 of a client's money in a bond deal on his very first day at work on the Street.

His voice dropping to what he thought was a whisper but was in fact still a shout, Smart said to Moore in Harry's Bar, "This stock will be the mudder of all winners, I'm telling you," mixing a little horse-racing talk with his stock market patter. "Tonight I will make you a rich man, Tom Moore."

The details: Smart's firm was coming out with the proverbial hot IPO. Ron wanted to offer Tom the golden once-in-a-lifetime opportunity to buy 10,000 shares of Sterling Homes at $20 each and turn them around in a couple of days for major money. Sterling Homes was a builder of modular homes.

Why not? Moore thought. He was raw, but he knew that this was the way it goes with IPOs. Some of his friends had already cashed in with these offerings. He knew that they were just about the most common inside play on the Street and were perfectly legal at that, usually. He had been wondering when his opportunity would come along. Here it was.

As Moore was mulling the offer, Smart announced one condition, the same one we just encountered in the story involving Jonathan Meaders and XXX Corp. Moore would have to buy an additional 20,000 shares of Sterling Homes when the stock hit the market on opening day.

Fine, Moore thought. This is the way it's done. This is the way brokers help each other. And the more shares I buy, the more I make. The big day arrived, and as predicted, Sterling Homes took off like a rocket instantly. The $20 initial price shot to $30 before Moore could buy his 20,000 shares. But he did buy them because he had said he would and because he already had a nice profit on the first 10,000 shares. On the third day of trading the stock closed at $49, and Moore was beside himself with joy when he made the announcement to his wife at their victory dinner.

They should have held off on that celebration. Within the first hour of trading on day 4, Sterling Homes plunged 10 points to $39. Everyone was cashing in. The underwriters and their minions hadn't been able to stoke the fire high enough and long enough. Now they were bailing out. This was, of course, a signal for the bears to awaken from their slumber and move in for the kill. It's a funny thing about these beasts. The professional bears can be in deep hibernation, apparently, but they spring for the kill at the slightest hint of blood. That was what happened here. The bogus bulls were selling. The bears were short selling. There weren't enough chumps buying. The stock fell through the floor. At $10, Sterling Homes no longer looked like such a golden opportunity to Moore. He hadn't been able to get out fast enough. But at least his wife was understanding. And so was Ron Smart, who was full of commiseration for his new friend's rotten luck. Smart himself, however, had escaped in fine shape.

And what about the company, Sterling Homes? Well, these things happen. Very regrettable. Soon enough the company went out of business.

Gross manipulation of the aftermarket on IPO shares violates securities laws. The underwriter D. H. Blair & Co., according to newspaper accounts, has been under investigation for four years by the Securities and Exchange Commission because of complaints about alleged noncompliance with federal securities laws regarding its IPO offerings. Some of the witnesses for stockholders and the SEC are former Blair employees. The company insists that it has done and is doing nothing wrong. It denies it has broken either the letter or the spirit of any securities laws.

There's no question that Blair takes a big position in the companies it takes public; the issue is whether the firm gets out of those stocks at much higher prices than its own clients, much less ordinary shareholders, do. In any event,

Blair, under the ownership of J. Morton Davis, has been one of the busiest underwriters on the Street since 1980.

I mentioned earlier that one way for underwriters to limit the all-important supply of shares for sale in the aftermarket (thus keeping the price as high as possible for as long as possible) is to limit such sell orders in some cases. These underwriters simply don't allow some of the small insiders to cash in when they want to. In effect, these smaller investors in the IPO are the last ones invited to the trough at cash-in time. This practice is one of the main complaints alleged against Blair. One instance in which such charges became public occurred in 1987, when Sidney Metzner and other Blair clients filed suit in Manhattan federal court, claiming that Blair steadfastly refused to sell its holdings, which they felt were eroding in value. The suit alleged that Blair liquidated the account only after the plaintiffs hired a lawyer, and at a loss of $160,000 to the investors. The suit alleged that Blair used the accounts of many of its clients "as a vehicle for generating a false appearance of activity in the respective securities underwritten by them." The action was settled without admitting liability for $125,000.

Kenton Wood, President of Blair, acknowledges that customers are encouraged to hold on to their shares in IPO offerings because that is the wisest investing strategy in the venture capital game. However, Wood states that customers must be able to sell their shares if they want to do so, wisely or unwisely, and goes on to say that customers of Blair are allowed to do so.

It is also alleged that Blair pressures not just smaller private investors but certain institutional investors—brokerage houses and mutual funds—to hold on to their shares. The source of Blair's power in these instances is alleged to be either his equity position in these firms or the fact that he has supported other companies' shares in which these institutional investors own big stakes. In effect, this is a case of I scratched your back, now you scratch mine. Indeed, no rules prohibit underwriters from holding an equity position in the brokerage firms that distribute their IPO offerings. The illegality would stem from using this relationship to manipulate the prices of the stocks. Among the investment companies alleged to be the subject of such pressure are F. N. Wolf & Co., Parliament Hill Capital Corp., and the now defunct J. T. Moran & Co. and R. H. Damon & Co. Among the mutual fund companies is Engex, Inc.

Morton Davis, owner of D. H. Blair, was also President of Engex in 1987 and 1989, when Engex was questioned about the fund's purchases of IPOs sponsored by Blair. Morton Davis was also a major shareholder in a now defunct securities firm named Broadchild Securities Corp., which was a big buyer of Blair's IPO offerings. A former president of Broadchild, Franklin Wolf, formed F. N. Wolf in 1982 and became a significant supporter and market maker for Blair-sponsored stocks. *Another* former Broadchild president was J. T. Moran, who left to form his own company and—you guessed it—also became a big pusher of Blair offerings.

Finally, Josephine Arcano, yet *another* of the founders of Broadchild Securities, filed a breach of contract suit against Morton Davis that involved the get-rich-quick approach that allegedly caused the demise of the company. Arcano alleged that Morty Davis openly asked a Broadchild employee to teach brokers "to buy highly risky securities so insiders, including Davis, would make a handsome profit before its price fell." She also claimed that Broadchild had been marketing at least 40 percent of Blair's initial public offerings and that at one time Blair had held on the order of $22 million in stock in companies the firm took public.

A jury awarded Arcano $3 million in damages. Before she collected that reward, the suit was settled out of court with Davis neither admitting nor denying liability for an undisclosed amount.

Now for some specific Blair windfalls. SEC filings show that Blair received convertible warrants to buy 180,000 shares of Xicor, a supplier of reprogrammable semiconductor memory products, at $7.80 a share when it took the company public in 1980. In March 1983 Blair exercised the warrants and sold the stock at $14.50 a share. Blair's profit: $1.2 million.

Certainly there's no crime in making a big profit from a stock, but questions are raised when the stock subsequently plummets. Xicor now sells for $2 a share.

Blair's critics—the plaintiffs in the lawsuits—also cite the performance of TIE/Communications, which Blair took public in 1979, retaining an 8 percent stake and warrants to buy 50,000 shares. Shares acquired at a cost of $100,000 were sold in 1986 for $35 million. That kind of profit raises eyebrows, even on Wall Street, when the company subsequently files for bankruptcy, which was TIE's situation in

1994. Even though this filing occurred 15 years after the IPO and could not be laid at Blair's doorstep, it always looks bad for the underwriter when a company it takes public goes under. The closer the bankruptcy to the IPO, the worse it looks.

After all the battles with bears and bulls and plaintiffs and their lawyers, Blair and its owner, Morton Davis, are still going strong. This fact leads to one of two conclusions. Either the company is wrongly vilified and is in fact a totally upright and efficient organization, or the whole IPO system stinks.

Your call.

The Chinese Wall

D o you need another case study before making your decision? Consider this fascinating episode involving a fledg-
ling outfit named Clinicorp, a company that at one time
owned and operated a chain of sixty-five chiropractic and
physical therapy clinics, mainly in Florida and Texas.
Clinicorp was the handiwork of one of the more resourceful
wheeler-dealers on Wall Street. His name is Robert Goldsamt,
and a little background on this investor is necessary.

A graduate of the Wharton School of Finance, Goldsamt
put in a brief stint as an investment banker before switch-
ing sides, as it were. His métier was founding small companies in the hospital management business and building them
into attractive takeover targets. Goldsamt was making deals
on the Street when Michael Milken was still in diapers
(okay, this is a slight exaggeration, but Goldsamt was enjoying tremendous success with buyouts in the 1960s). His

main claim to fame is American Medicorp, one of the earliest of these health management companies, founded in the 1960s. It eventually became the country's second largest operator of acute-care hospitals and was acquired by Humana, Inc., in 1977.

With that and other health care successes under his belt and goaded in part by the bear market in the middle 1970s that crimped the entire buyout industry, particularly in the health care field, Goldsamt switched his attention to retailing and distribution. Eventually he founded Integrated Barter, Inc., in 1982, and then, in 1983, he decided to take public the retailing arm of Integrated Barter. The idea was that the new Closeouts Plus Co. Inc. would run a chain of discount stores in the New York area.

It almost happened, but on the very day when the $8 million IPO was supposed to be launched, the parent company reported losses for the quarter, as well as an unexpected write-off. The SEC stopped the offering and conducted an inquiry into this IPO, concluding that something was rotten somewhere. The SEC charged the parent company with failure to disclose fully its own financial problems in the prospectus for the spun-off company. The initial offering had been fully subscribed; all trades had to be rescinded. Goldsamt settled all the charges resulting from this debacle but did not admit any malfeasance.

Now we come back to Clinicorp. In 1990 Goldsamt realized that there was money to be made treating a nation of bad backs covered by health insurance. (There was little money to be made treating a nation of bad backs that were not covered by health insurance.) Goldsamt and his crew joined a licensed chiropractor named Peter G. Fernandez in founding Clinicorp, and this management team immediately went to a small Wall Street investment bank named RAS Securities for some money.

RAS was a willing underwriter. Its analysts identified the chiropractic industry as a $7 billion to $10 billion gold mine. RAS's president, Bob Schneider, brought out all the firm's big guns to promote Clinicorp to its major clients. After all, chiropractic treatment was "the third largest primary health care profession in the western world, after medicine and dentistry" (a strange come-on when you stop to think about it, but there you are).

The biggest of all the big guns called in by RAS was Raymond Dirks, the legendary expert on the insurance industry who gained nationwide fame in 1973 when he blew the whistle on Equity Funding Co., a California insurer that was cooking its books at a very high temperature. Almost twenty years later Dirks was now the principal at Ray Dirks Research, a unit of RAS Securities. His assign-ment this time was to sing a different kind of tune.

For starters, he estimated that Clinicorp's annualized rev-enues could exceed $120 million, with an earning power of $3.50 a share. He went on to suggest that if Clinicorp could incorporate orthopedic surgeons into its chiropractic net-work and thus gain control of back pain claims within state workers' compensation systems, it could corner the market on this significant portion of the $70 billion workers' com-pensation industry.

Because of Dirks's personal credibility, this kind of rec-ommendation created a high level of credibility for

Clinicorp. On January 13, 1992, Goldsamt's latest venture went public with a fully subscribed IPO worth $6.5 million, plus another $18 million garnered from a private sale of 1.7 million shares to Sands Brothers, another smallish New York investment and securities firm. Add in the extra IPO shares that could be issued to the underwriter—the over-allotment, as it's called—and the total sum raised for Clinicorp on January 13 was nearly $30 million. Not bad at all for a company with no assets to speak of. Clinicorp had yet to acquire its first clinic.

Initially priced at $6.50, the stock began a steady ascent propelled by Raymond Dirks's reputation, RAS analysts' projections of a $50 trading price when the company got up to speed in a couple of years, and the incessant drumming of RAS's brokers. One year after the IPO, Clinicorp stock was still trading at $18 even though it had not yet earned its first dime.

Then reality set in. With IPOs this inevitably happens sooner or later (and usually, but not always, on the down-side). In the latter half of 1993 Clinicorp's auditors raised a warning flag that was based on their assessment of the company's May 31 financial statement, which reported revenues of $5.3 million and a net loss of $11.3 million, or $1.10 a share, for fiscal 1993.

Soon enough Clinicorp stock had skidded to the $5 range, and investors were reacting to more than just the auditor's report. Yes, the company had acquired thirty-five chiropractic clinics and five rehabilitation centers, but it had paid for those purchases with money gained by selling 8 mil-lion shares in private placements for $22 million. Those sales were never publicly announced and were not widely known. By the end of 1993 the number of outstanding shares of Clinicorp had ballooned from a reasonable 2.5 million to an enormous 21 million. (A standard offering for newly trading companies would be 5 million to 10 million shares.) Astute shareholders understood that the result of this largesse would be a significant dilution of stock earnings when and if there were any stock earnings.

Still, upbeat prognostications continued. Michael M. LeConey, an analyst at Ray Dirks Research (a wing of RAS Securities, the underwriting firm), declared on July 15 that the company was "emerging from the inevitable shakeout phase that accompanies the development of the right format, management team, and general strategy to optimize a major opportunity." Therefore, LeConey continued, Clinicorp "is on the verge of achieving operating profitability together with the extraordinary growth that is characteristic of a company in its takeoff growth phase."

The analyst estimated that Clinicorp would earn 50 cents to $1 a share in the fiscal year ending May 30, 1994, and could reach $1.50 to $2.50 in fiscal 1995. LeConey concluded, "At $5.25 a share, the stock is one of the few truly outstanding opportunities in the health care service area. Our near-term target price is $10 a share. Longer term we look for $30 to $45 a share."

The analyst's report did not mention the private placements. (Such reports usually do and should.)

One week later RAS analyst Thomas Heysek was equally bullish. He said that the company had gone through restructuring to cut costs and speed up acquisitions. He predicted that the management team would be "leaner and more focused and more determined" under a new CEO. Finally he stated, "Clinicorp is an exceptional investment opportunity."

This report didn't mention the private placements either.

Despite these two glowing predictions, shareholders and prospective shareholders failed to carry the torch. The bulls ignored Clinicorp. On August 19 the financial journalist Dan Dorfman, then with *USA Today* and now with *Money* magazine, suggested on his cable television show that Clinicorp could be in trouble. Just one month after the company received those two glowing reports by in-house analysts, Dorfman said, "I am hearing that the company cannot account for some money and that the company may go bankrupt."

A company spokesperson referred to that rumor as "baloney."

What about any missing money? Indeed, it wasn't entirely clear where the initial $30 million had gone. It had not gone to buy the clinics, which were paid for by those private placements, and the company could not possibly have spent $30 million on operating costs. One thing was certain: The Dorfman remark had killed for the moment all hopes of going back to the venture capital market for another $10 million, which had been the plan. In fact, an offering for $2 million was already in the planning stages. That had to be called off abruptly.

Late in that year, 1993, Goldsamt appointed Tim McMillen as chief administrative officer in charge of acquisitions. McMillen was a former representative from Mary-

land, and he explained that his new employer had been subject to a "bear raid orchestrated by several disgruntled former employees." McMillen insisted that all funds from the
IPO (and the private placements) had been handled properly and could be accounted for.

(Well, maybe.) McMillen's report stated that $28 million
had been devoured by "company expenses," including $16
million classified as "operational costs." Of this $16 million,
about $5 million was spent on "professional fees" and $8
million was assigned to "other expenses."

Then, early in 1994, Clinicorp management announced
a restructuring and the termination of certain contracts; it
also recognized losses from the disposition of underper-
forming clinics and the settlement of outstanding litigation.
The result was an unbelievable balance sheet showing current assets of $11.5 million, liabilities of just $5 million,
long-term debt of only $2.2 million, and an astounding net
worth of $28 million.

Justifiably, the market was not convinced. The stock was
trading in the $2 range. More important for management
was the question of how the company would survive the
financial straits it had created for itself. Then Goldsamt and
team had a brainstorm: purchase a health maintenance organization (HMO). This primary-care HMO would be a
dependable source of patients for the chiropractic clinics. In
February the company announced the acquisition of a
Florida-based HMO for $27 million in cash and stocks.

And where were the cash and stocks to come from? Wall
Street.

Fundamental logic says that this company, which had obtained almost $30 million since the IPO in 1992, with no earnings to show for it two years later, may be targeted for the waste bin. Fundamental *Wall Street* logic—sometimes a very different thing—said that the answer to Clinicorp's problem was to finagle another $40 million or $50 million in capitalization with the help of the people who had raised the first $30 million. An impossible dream? By no means. As one of his goons, Rocko, told Michael Corleone in *The Godfather, Part II* regarding their prospects for knocking off former associate Hyman Roth, "Difficult but not impossible."

According to an individual close to the negotiations for that new underwriting, plan A called for buying the HMO for Clinicorp shares (again), while plan B advocated going straight to the public for another offering of $50 million worth of stock and using this cash to buy the HMO.

Give the preliminary prospectus for this new offering credit for honesty (although some such statement would be required by the SEC): "The company has limited revenues, a history of losses, negative cash flow, and there is doubt as to its ability to continue as a going concern."

If the offering had gone through, a list of the new crop of investors would have made interesting reading. Already interesting is the published list of parties who would be *selling* their shares of Clinicorp: those investors who snapped up shares in what may turn out to be ill-fated private placements at prices ranging from $2 to $7; Robert Schneider, the president of RAS Securities and the prime mover behind the first IPO and this additional offering; Richard Sands, managing director of Sands Brothers & Co., which was instrumental in the private placements; Oppenheimer Discovery Fund and Oppenheimer Time Fund; Michael LeConey, the stubbornly bullish analyst; and Ray Dirks, whose zealous touting got Clinicorp off the ground in the first place. Of course, Robert Goldsamt will reduce his stake in the company to 11 percent.

Despite everything concerning Clinicorp, some Street insiders thought that the company and its friends on Wall Street might well bring home the new bacon. Forget the doomed $30 million. Wall Street delivers for its closest and dearest friends.

Or at least it tries to. In the case of Clinicorp it did not succeed. By September 1994, 12 cents would have made you a proud shareholder. The American Stock Exchange succumbed to the inevitable and stopped trading in the stock until the company filed its annual report with the SEC. The company said that it would file by September 12 but failed to meet that date, although it announced that the number of clinics in its stable was down to thirty-five from a high of sixty-five and stated that it expected to report a net loss of $34 million for the year ended May 31 (compared to an $11.3 million loss the year before).

In light of these factors, which no amount of hyping and bullish analysts' reports could overcome, RAS Securities dropped all plans for another underwriting for Clinicorp, nor would the SEC ever approve such an offering. But regardless of what happens with Clinicorp, don't shed tears for Robert Goldsamt. There's no indication at all that the founder has suffered financially because of his company's travail. If you believe that's the case or even *might be* the case, you know nothing about high finance on Wall Street, where one can make a lot of money in the course of bringing down a company and losing one's own job.

The original Chinese wall, which was built of stone and earth over 2,000 years ago, was an impressive piece of work. Fourteen hundred miles long and at least twenty feet high, it proved to be a formidable defense against invading warriors. We wouldn't expect anything quite so strong to enforce regulations and ethics on Wall Street, but the barrier separating the underwriters in Wall Street securities firms from the analysts and brokers is supposed to be stout. The two "sides" are never supposed to share information regarding upcoming underwritings. The idea is to avoid any opportunity for trading on inside information regarding IPOs and any opportunity for setting up cozy and unethical relationships.

Funniest thing, though. As we have just witnessed in the notorious example of Clinicorp, the Wall Street barrier is somewhat more porous than its namesake in Asia. On Wall Street the term "Chinese wall" is used only with the tongue planted firmly in the cheek. On Wall Street the wall might as well be made of the paper used in Chinese lanterns.

The truth is that the left hand of an investment house knows *exactly* what the right hand is doing. In many cases they shake on the deal! In fact, securities analysts have become one of the linchpins in the world of corporate finance. Analysts on the sixteenth floor have become business solicitors for the investment bankers on the seventeenth floor. The companies the analysts cover become prime candidates for in-house underwriting work.

What's the big problem with this arrangement? Simple: It can and does lead to the temptation for full-service securities firms to create or at least imply this kind of "synergy": "You let us do some underwriting or other financial jobs for your company, and in return we'll see to it that your company gets a good rating in our analysts' reports."

When events turn out as they did in the Clinicorp fiasco and when much of the hype that boosted the stock in the first place is of the in-house variety, questions of propriety and ethics are inevitable. Both the *inter*house conflicts of interest we observed in the discussion of D. H. Blair & Co. and the *intra*house conflicts of interest we saw at RAS Securities are pernicious.

The incestuous relationship between analysts and underwriters is about as slippery and unethical as it gets on Wall Street—and under certain circumstances may lead to illegal acts, too. But it's common practice. It's also common practice for an analyst who has helped bring in an underwriting client to get a considerable slice of that more than considerable underwriting fee. This analyst then does the basic number crunching on this new offering—gee, the arithmetic usually comes out looking pretty optimistic. Then the analyst undertakes the yeoman's job of selling the new stock to the other part of the market, the investors.

Thus this stalwart of Wall Street, the securities analyst who is theoretically devoted to the objective assessment of his or her companies, totally sealed off from the rest of the firm in a selfless search for good stock opportunities, is in actuality *just the opposite*. The analyst's real job is to find as many underwriting and corporate finance clients as possible. The winner gets a big bonus. By this I don't mean a seven-day holiday cruise to Puerto Vallarta; more likely is a seven-*figure* check in the Christmas stocking.

Surely I exaggerate? Surely the episodes are fairly rare? If you think so, contemplate the words of the director of research—the chief analyst!—at a major Wall Street firm. This man frankly acknowledges that he has been told in no uncertain terms "to deliver the clients—or else. Those who lag in this contest end up in the company doghouse—if not out the door completely."

There are a few exceptions to the rule. Some investment houses actually have constructed some kind of meaningful Chinese wall. These model citizens of Wall Street either have such a good investment business going that they don't need to engage in unethical practices or are so small and puny that they can't compete head to head with the big dogs and don't even try.

Overall, this issue of the incestuous relationship between the underwriters and the analysts will get worse, not better, as competition for underwriting jobs gets tougher, thanks in part to the encroachment of the commercial banks on what used to be the exclusive turf of the investment firms. Regulations promulgated in recent years already allow commercial banks to provide corporate investment advice and indirectly sell mutual funds. It's only a matter of time before the Glass-Steagall Act, which bars commercial banks from providing corporate securities underwriting, is dismantled by Congress. When that happens—and the question is when, not if—all hell will break loose in this, the most lucrative of all Wall Street activities. Then you'll need a Ph.D. in archaeology to find the buried remains of the Chinese wall in the most respected and upright firms.

Heavenly Designs

don't want to give you the impression that every single public offering is greeted with open arms by the insiders. There are limits. Sometimes even well-known brand-name offerings run into problems. Donna Karan is one of the more recent cases in point. Her world-famous company creates and then contracts for the manufacturing and distribution of men's and women's designer lines, the most famous of which is the ubiquitous DKNY. The most prestigious department and specialty stores in America are Karan's customers. Saks Fifth Avenue accounts for 11 percent of her revenues—not surprising, perhaps, since sexy DKNY advertisements are featured on almost every bus and bus stop in Manhattan. Neiman Marcus and Bergdorf Goodman account for another 14 percent of DKNY sales. From 1986 to 1992 revenues grew at a compounded rate of 54 percent, from $19 million to $260 million. Operating revenues jumped from $54,000 to $33 million six years later.

By any definition, this is fast-track growth. What Donna wants on Seventh Avenue, Donna gets. So she and her team at DKNY were perhaps surprised to learn that her famous and profitable apparel business carries a good deal more clout in the designer district on Seventh Avenue than it does several miles to the south, in the financial district on Wall Street, where celebrity usually counts for a great deal. And the most shocked of all might have been Karan's personal astrologer and soothsayer, without whose blessing the famous designer does not turn one hem, or so word on the Street has it. If astrology is good enough for Nancy Reagan, why not for Donna Karan?

Early in 1994 Donna was convinced that this was the right time to turn her life's work into a publicly traded company and also to buy out her Japanese partners, the Takihyo Group, which provided $2 million in seed money back in 1985. Donna Karan's astrologer not only agreed with her boss that an IPO from DKNY had the blessing of the stars and the planets but went so far as to say, "It must happen."

In the DKNY shop this endorsement usually seals the deal. But not in this case. Neither the principal nor her astrologer counted on the stubborn opposition of none other than Stephan Weiss, Karan's strong-willed husband, vice chairman, and co-CEO.

"Not this year," Weiss barked. He was concerned that the offering would not receive its true valuation because of a couple of "little problems." From the time the IPO venture had been planned under the auspices of Bear Stearns and Morgan Stanley in 1993, the company had posted lower than expected sales and earnings for that year: earnings of $30 million on sales of more than $300 million. The initial plan had called for issuing 11 million shares at an initial price of $16. Weiss feared that the latest report would lower those numbers.

Another perceived problem was the upscale orientation of DKNY's apparel. The idea of a cashmere-spandex body suit going for $800 and a partially lined wool blazer costing $1,400 concerned some institutional investors. Such prices were headed in the wrong direction. The apparel industry as a whole was on the ropes, and the public was moving toward discounted goods at discount stores. Could DKNY buck the trend?

Some IPO pros also frowned on the way in which the deal was structured. Specifically, Karan and Weiss would continue to own certain trademarks, including Donna Karan New York and DKNY, and so they would collect millions in royalties from the revenue stream. There was concern that such an arrangement might discourage the principals from exerting a maximum effort toward improving profitability.

One portfolio manager, Kurt Winters with IDS Securities, was reported by *Business Week* marketing and fashion editor Laura Zinn to have thrown his DKNY prospectus in the trash. Winters told Zinn, "This IPO was primarily seen as a vehicle for Donna and her husband to cash out."

That goes without saying with many IPOs, which are without a doubt the best way for the founder and/or owner of a small or midcapitalized business to reap his, her, or their just rewards. And money is definitely important to both Donna Karan and Stephan Weiss. But don't underestimate the importance for Donna Karan of her astrologer's enthusiastic recommendation. That meant a great deal to Karan too.

Alas, the astrologer's seal of approval meant nothing to Stephan Weiss. The two spouses and business partners had a heated battle about the timing of the IPO. Donna wanted to heed the judgment of the astrologer; Stephan wanted to wait. It was that classic, age-old New Age confrontation on the Street: astrology versus economics and finance.

The underwriters were also expressing doubts about the timing of the DKNY IPO, but they would heed the wishes of their clients. Naturally. Finally, Donna Karan gave in and postponed the offering until autumn 1994 at the earliest. She was hard pressed to mollify her miffed stargazer.

As it turned out, perhaps the astrologer was correct. An early 1994 IPO would have corresponded nicely with a strong surge in the markets. The stock could have positioned itself before the 10 percent pullback in late March.

By late 1994 there was still no word about the reintroduced DKNY IPO, but Stephan Weiss told *Business Week* that "he isn't closing the door" to a public offering, although the company was able to obtain a $125 million credit facility from a syndicate of five financial institutions.

Weiss says that like many people, Donna Karan has an interest in astrology. But he rejects the notion that it plays any part in her design decisions or the company's business. "Ms. Karan's inspirations come not from the stars, but rather from what her customers say they need and want in terms of fashion," insists Weiss.

It's easy—it's tempting, in fact—to have a little fun with the idea of astrologers making crucial decisions for $300 million companies. However, oracle investing, as it's called, is not that quirky a practice on the Street. A number of market analysts use stargazing and planetary wobbles in forecasting market behavior. After all, why wouldn't such methods produce results at least on a par with those from dart throwing? Any number of comprehensive studies have shown that dart throwing yields a portfolio just about as productive as the average mutual fund. If you really have an inside track with the heavens, maybe you should play it for all it's worth.

One market pro who does just that, who makes no pretenses about his arcane analyses, is a serious-looking man named Arch Crawford—not a pseudonym, because Arch has nothing to hide. *Barron's* has labeled him the Street's best known astrologer. He has been in the investment management business for twenty-eight years, and he proudly proclaims that his buy and sell recommendations are based mainly on highly technical analyses of the interfaces of the orbits of the moon, the planets, and the stars. And don't forget solar flares and sunspot activity, which cause disruptive magnetic storms that exert an influence on human beings, just as they do on the tides. And anything which influences human beings en masse necessarily influences the stock markets.

In 1977 Crawford registered with the SEC as an investment adviser and started the newsletter *Crawford Perspectives*. He has devised a forecasting concept that calculates percentage changes in the Dow Jones back to the late 1800s, relates them to astronomical events, and fits them into a "cycles prediction line." Like any self-respecting market analyst, Crawford is always ready to whip out his list of triumphs. For the first half of 1994 Crawford Perspectives was ranked fourth among the sixty-six stock market advisory publications compared by the *Hulbert Financial Digest*. For the two-year period of 1991–1992 Crawford was judged the best "Long-Term Timer" by the *Timer Digest*, another publication that monitors investment advisers and market newsletters. For those two years the Standard & Poors 500-stock index gained 31.9 percent. Crawford trumped that at 37.4 percent.

But none of Crawford's claims to fame can surpass the call he issued in August 1987, when he informed his clients that the heavens were signaling a gigantic market collapse. "Our long-term sell signal is set in stone," the newsletter stated. "Be out of all stocks by August 24, from which point we expect a horrendous crash."

Less than two months later, on October 19, it happened.

However, Arch is the first to admit that the system doesn't always work. "As powerful as astronomy is," he explains, "it is still in a very early developmental stage, and it pays to keep two fingers on the pulse of the market through technical analysis." That's why he also tracks twenty-eight market indicators to augment his astronomical observations.

Crawford got his start in the field while a technical analyst at Merrill Lynch, where he was introduced to the work of one of the pacesetters in the field, Lieutenant Commander David Williams, who focused mainly on planetary positions. Then there was John Nelson, a radio propagation specialist for RCA in the 1940s, who correlated these planetary positions with the sun's surface and was able to predict the onset of sunspots and solar flares and the resulting magnetic storms.

Arch explains, "Stocks would drop sharply during those storms, and often gold would rally violently." He insists that it's a matter of history that "the largest modern burst of electrons from the sun's surface coincided with the week of the stock market crash in 1987 and also with a spectacular heliocentric alignment of the planets."

And Arch made the correct call on Black Monday.

It's not surprising that the media love this offbeat market maven. Everyone from *The Wall Street Journal* to ABC's *20/20* to Geraldo Rivera wants to know what Arch thinks about the market and about other matters. On June 30, 1990, the market's favorite stargazer predicted that something big was going to happen somewhere in the world between August 2 and August 7 of that year. Crawford couldn't specify exactly what this event would be, but he said, "The involvement of Mars and Pluto indicates an attempt at coercion, the use of force, and a powerful explosion. Venus opposing Saturn suggests heartlessness and cruelty."

On August 2, Iraq invaded Kuwait. The market went south.

In early January 1994 Crawford warned his readers that a "rare four-planet alignment would occur between September 18 and September 22, which would precipitate a very rapid stock market correction with perhaps international consequences."

On September 21 the Dow fell sixty-seven points, the third largest drop of the year since the general retreat that started on March 20.

Mere coincidence? A self-fulfilling prophecy, given Crawford's growing following? Perhaps and perhaps, but the astrologer and the readers who trust his judgments have been doing quite well in recent years. And you have to say this on behalf of Crawford's unique sort of inside information: It's not underhanded, it's not sneaky, and it's not illegal. That makes it positively refreshing.

The Mark of Soros

On one of his visits to London early in 1994 the legendary investor and guru of the financial markets George Soros was greeted at Heathrow Airport by a black limousine carrying a representative of the chancellor of the exchequer, an impressive display of the Hungarian's clout on the world financial scene. By consensus, in fact, Soros is the most influential *nongovernment* financial leader in the world. He is by now acclimated to regal treatment from governments worldwide, in part because of his power over financial markets and in part because of his well-known philanthropic generosity in at least nineteen different countries.

Of course, Soros's success in the financial markets (and most other markets) feeds his generosity, but another question inevitably surfaces: Does the generosity also feed the success? Has George Soros become the quintessential glob-

al insider trader by exploiting contacts and friends in government circles to gain access to what is otherwise inacces-
sible information?

This definitely *could be* the case. As we have seen, laws
against insider trading in the United States are remarkably
porous, but at least there are such laws and at least they are
enforced at some times and in some places. Overseas, it's a
different matter. Sanctions against insider trading are
loosely applied in most other nations, although Germany
has recently taken steps to form an SEC-type agency to
police its markets.

We can go back to 1977 to find out at least one reason
why this is the case, one reason why Soros might not be
fond of the stock markets in the United States. In fact, a former adviser says bluntly that the global investment guru is
not known for his stock picking skills. (That said, it must be
acknowledged that Soros did predict the crash in the
Japanese market well in advance of that 1989 debacle.)

This former adviser happens to be one of those well-
placed investors who were instrumental in setting up
Soros's worldwide network of insider information. He was
hired specifically to help Soros open the heaviest doors in
certain European countries, and he thinks his former
employer's aversion to stocks may date from an encounter
with the Securities and Exchange Commission in 1977 concerning the sale of a large block of shares in Computer
Sciences. This happened on the day before the company
issued a new public offering. The big Soros sale pushed the
stock down 50 cents to $8.37 a share. Soros then started
buying at that level, purchasing 165,000 shares in all.

The SEC alleged that Soros had manipulated the stock. To avoid any legal proceedings against him, he signed a consent decree—that infamous legal document which neither admits nor denies guilt. But then the Fletcher Jones Foundation, one of the major investors that had taken a bath on Computer Sciences, sued Soros and agreed to a $1 million out-of-court settlement. Since then Soros has preferred more "out of the way" trading. Clear over the horizon. Overseas.

The heart of the Soros operation is the Quantum Group, with assets of $10 billion. Quantum speculates and trades aggressively in currencies, bonds, commodities, all kinds of exotic derivatives of securities, and interest rate plays. The staff of fourteen incredibly savvy traders works in New York City, but legally, Quantum Group is anchored offshore. This setup carries the disadvantage of making the fund unavailable to American investors. However, this drawback is far outweighed by the fact that the offshore setting also puts Quantum beyond the reach of American securities laws.

Writing in *The New York Times Magazine* in April 1994, Lyle Crowley called Soros "the consummate insider . . . something of a renegade in the financial world, a risk-taker so daring that even members of Congress are trying to figure out exactly how his game works."

The details of his investing techniques are vague, but this much is certain: Thanks to his "overseas" standing, Soros is free to make use of his unparalleled network of contacts, which reaches so high that the word "contact" becomes an understatement. His best sources include decision makers at the Office of the Exchequer in London, the Bundesbank in

Frankfurt, and other vital financial centers around the globe. This kind of insider network takes Soros way beyond mere "connections." No wonder he's the envy of Wall Street in this regard.

His uttered word and his fiercely forward trading can become a self-fulfilling prophecy, and a dangerous one at that. On August 4, 1993, Soros publicly announced his displeasure with the British pound. The currency was highly overvalued and headed for a major fall, he said. He announced his intention to sell pounds and load up on dollars. Predictably, the financial markets instantly lost confidence in the pound, and the currency plunged. The Bank of England nearly went broke in its efforts to prop up its favorite currency. Fed up, the British government subsequently abandoned the European exchange rate system rather than continue to defend the pound through interventions in the currency markets.

Meanwhile, the financier left his indelible "mark of Soros" when he sauntered away from the scene with a cool $1 billion profit because he was the first out of the skidding pound and the first into the rising dollar.

Soros's throng of admirers and his public relations team swung into action, crediting the audacious bet against the pound to the boss's genius and prescient reading of Britain's fundamental economic and monetary condition. Perhaps. Others suspect that Soros had some help in engineering that self-fulfilling prophecy. And possibly, they say that one of Soros' "very deep" sources in the Exchequer's lair had tipped him that the British pound would soon come under

extreme pressure because Britain would not be able to operate within the European monetary system. In addition, the
sentiment among currency speculators was that if the
British pound is not included in the European Monetary
System, demand for the pound will not be robust when
stacked up against that for the other EMS currencies.

Soros's announcement and lightning-swift trading move
served to trigger the crisis, as he must have known it would.
As Lyle Crowley also wrote in *The New York Times*, Soros
is the ultimate insider but is also "the quintessential outsider, the contrarian who makes fortunes by betting on the
demise of others."

As *Business Week* said in a cover story, he is "the scourge
of Europe's central banks" whose pronouncements "make
the government bankers cringe—particularly in Europe,
where exchange-rate mechanisms force them onto the opposing side of Soros's trades, and where, more often than not,
they wind up as losers."

We know that Soros has the best of connections. That's
one of his secrets. Another, he says, is his frankly pessimistic
assessment of human nature and human decision making.
His brand of "contrarian" investing is based on a concept he
describes as "reflexivity," which argues that human decisions are usually flawed.

He told *Business Week*, "The key insight that I have
reached is recognition of the inherent fallibility of human
thought."

Soros's book *The Alchemy of Finance* is devoted entirely
to this provocative if ancient theory. It follows that all the

flawed human decisions in economic matters produce major misperceptions regarding the markets and, consequently, boom and bust cycles. His only advantage in the battle of wits to take advantage of these cycles, Soros told *Business Week,* is that he recognizes his own propensity to error. A grin spread across his tanned face as he quipped that "amateurs like us" can't be expected to know where the world's financial markets are headed in 1994 or any other year.

"I make as many mistakes as the next guy," he said.

Perhaps. But one mistake Soros does *not* make is to go into situations half-cocked. He does not bet the bank with iffy information. His favorite theory may or may not hold water, but what Soros has that the next guy unquestionably does *not* have is that deep source in the office of the exchequer in London.

So far, the sixty-three-year-old Hungarian's system and network have worked superbly. And then, when things do go awry, well, the theory predicts that many human judgments will be in error. In this enviable win-win situation, Soros's reputation can remain untarnished. It did so in February 1994, when President Clinton and Prime Minister Hosokawa were engaged in bilateral trade discussions. The going was heavy. Soros determined that the impending collapse of the talks would be good news for the dollar at the expense of the yen. Soros bought dollars and sold yen, a typically Sorosistic plunge, but this time with no input from the Japanese, with no insider tips from anyone.

Alas, this was one of those errors that are inevitable in human affairs. The yen actually firmed up against the dollar, partly because Japanese investors and other trade experts viewed the United States–Japan discord as a positive boost to Japan's exports and the Japanese economy as a whole. No mark of Soros this time. The Hungarian savant emerged from that shoot-out about $600 million in the red. But maybe that was appropriate for Valentine's Day.

The Regs on Reg-S

ithout a doubt, the woman I will call "Walda Walling" is one of the unique characters making a great deal of money on Wall Street in the 1990s. She's no George Soros, accustomed to dining with prime ministers and their principal advisers, but Walda's five-person firm, headquartered in Manhattan, posted earnings of several million dollars in 1993 from underwriting operations. What's so unusual about that? Nothing. But what is unusual about the firm is that the boss has neither the credentials nor the license to put together corporate underwritings or practice investment banking. Nor is Walda a licensed broker, or a registered representative of any brokerage firm. Who or what is Walda Walling, and how does she produce such underwriting results?

Well, she's a freelance stock market operator who gets around the little problem of licenses by plying her trade offshore, where she doesn't need the permission of the SEC. Shades of Soros. And one other thing, which Soros cannot match. While anyone who has met Walda immediately acknowledges her diligence and shrewdness and innate intelligence—in this regard she's more than a match for well-seasoned, top-of-the-line investment bankers—Walda admits without embarrassment that she wields a secret weapon. When push comes to shove, she'll lay her ace on the bargaining table. Walda, you see, will do *anything* to close a deal.

"Timing is everything, as the Street traders say," Walda tells me as I ask her about her precious key to success. "First," she says, "I make a point to ask the critical questions about a deal—any particular project I may have cooking in the oven—at the most precise time."

She recalls one time when she met a European financial titan for the first time at a regal banquet marking his company's 20th anniversary, this baron of mutual funds couldn't take his eyes off Walda, although he had his wife in his arms. He and his wife were on the dance floor at the time. Walda knew who he was, of course, and the main purpose of her attending the exquisite dinner affair was to be able to talk to him about a stock that she had called him about when she was in New York. A friend in Germany introduced Walda on the phone.

Walda remembers that when he found the opportunity to break away from his wife that evening, he quickly approached her and made his move, in his most charming manner. He assured her that, yes, he liked the Reg-S stock Walda was pitching, and could they meet at her hotel one hour before midnight "to close the deal"?

Needless to say, Walda was waiting for him on the hour before midnight. They ultimately found themselves romancing on the sofa, and, as Walda recalls, that was the occasion when she raised the *key* question at the right time. At the precise time that he pulled her to him and put his mouth on hers, Walda whispered sweetly but very clearly, "Are you really going to buy one million shares of 'Lightning Casino'?" Walda got the answer she wanted, and they consummated the deal. "My system works, simple as it is," says Walda, obviously content with the way she handles business.

She clinches a deal better that way, she asserts, while avoiding any appearance of a quid pro quo. Is it going too far to call the heroine of this chapter, this never-married, workaholic, attractive brunette in her middle thirties, a Mistress of the Universe?

In 1993 Walda raised $55 million for fifteen companies, and her system is simple: She takes advantage of the huge European, Asian, and Middle Eastern appetite for American stocks by going directly to those big overseas investors. By now—after five years in private practice—she has quite a network of institutions and high-rolling individuals overseas who are ready and willing to deal with her. She considers her activities no different from the private placements set up by the registered brokerage houses.

Now meet a man I call "Franz Munster," a financial fox who owns and operates a chain of mutual funds all over Europe with assets of several billion dollars. These funds daily buy and sell stocks worth up to $2 million, making the funds and their owner a huge force in European financial circles. Munster operates like a recluse. He meets only a handful of money managers or clients every week in his mansionlike offices. He rarely entertains, and when he does so, the private dinners have the air of serious business meetings. It almost goes without saying that he is well connected in the highest levels of European government.

Franz and his mutual funds no doubt own hundreds of thousands of shares of giants such as Philip Morris, Microsoft, General Motors, and Coca-Cola as well as shares of the equivalent stock market prima donnas of Europe. But this conservative and prudent investor also has a passion for speculative, low-priced, and largely ignored U.S. companies. This is the area in which he looks for his most exciting and profitable opportunities, and indeed he has generated phenomenal returns of 35 to 100 percent from these Small-Cap stocks trading on the Nasdaq market.

And this titan of European mutual fund operators gives all the credit in this area to his "stock goddess," the one and only Walda Walling.

Franz is Walda's biggest client in Europe; Walda is Franz's principal supplier of U.S securities. And what securities can deliver such returns for Walda's chosen clients? Reg-S stocks, as they are called, which is short for Regulation S. These are Walda's stock in trade. They are unregistered shares that don't have to be reported to or listed with the Securities and Exchange Commission. They cannot be legally purchased by American citizens. Most important of all, they are priced at a discount ranging from 10 to 50 percent.

I should make clear that Regulation S, which was drafted by the SEC in 1990, is quite different from Rule 144, which regulates the purchase and sale of unregistered securities *in this country*. These are the private placements I have mentioned several times in this book, a very handy play for corporate insiders—and corporate insiders only. These placements are usually for stock options priced at a modest discount from a stock's market price at the time. They cannot be sold for two years from the date of purchase. In this regard they're way behind the times compared with Regulation S transactions. Reg-S stocks can be turned within forty days, and you can bet that they are.

Reg-S stocks are a great insiders' play. The intention of Regulation S as drafted by the SEC is to provide foreign investors with convenient access to American securities at the least cost to those companies. Reg-S accomplishes this goal very well. But meanwhile, the domestic shareholders of American companies that issue Reg-S stocks are at a double disadvantage. First, these investors have to pay more for their shares. Second, they do not know how many Reg-S shares have been sold overseas through this unregulated window and therefore do not know the extent of the dilution of the earnings per share. Just about the only way for the average investor to get even a hint that something is afoot overseas is to watch a company's number of shares outstanding. If the number rises suddenly—within a week, say, or perhaps a month—and without explanation from the corporation, you have probably just "witnessed" the issuance and sale of a batch of Reg-S stocks.

Read it and weep. You were never given the opportunity to buy those shares at such a steep discount.

And then watch what happens to the price of the stock. It sags. Why? Many overseas investors who are about to buy Reg-S shares *short the stock* beforehand, intending to use the deeply discounted Reg-S shares to fulfill their obligation on the short side. Sell at market price, buy at a deep discount. Presto! This is another guaranteed market miracle for the insiders, while the locked-out average investor sees the stock price fall as a result of the short selling. In fact, this investor is twice burned: The earnings per share for the stock are diluted, and the price of that share on the market goes down.

Make no mistake. This practice of shorting and using Reg-S shares to fulfill an obligation is absolutely illegal, even when practiced by overseas traders. Walda is one pro who cares very little about the issue of shorting, but many of the managers and traders who specialize in Reg-S stocks condemn the practice. Many of them even insist that their buyers hold on to their shares even after the forty-day restriction. But the practice goes on, of course, with or without the knowledge of the brokers who sold the shares, and you can bet that Americans have figured a way to carve out their share of this overseas bonanza. Some American investors who have the wherewithal have formed offshore companies that use foreign nominees to buy and sell Reg-S shares.

Reg-S schemes are so common that one Reg-S pro, Carol Martino, president of CMS Ltd., fears that the short sellers will kill the party for everyone else. Martino is sometimes called the queen of Reg-S; she claims that she makes it a condition of Reg-S purchases that her clients use them as a long-term tool. If the shorting practice by others does not stop, Martino fears, the SEC may shut down the whole Reg-S business. Martino is aware that a silent SEC probe of the Reg-S "industry" is under way with the goal of developing mechanisms to defeat, or at least minimize, the fraud while saving this means of raising capital.

The initial idea behind Regulation S was that it would help large, healthy corporations raise capital by selling stocks and bonds overseas. In practice, however, most of the companies that take advantage of the Reg-S window are small and medium-sized firms that need financing to achieve their production and earnings goals. The question for these companies becomes: Is it worth attracting foreign investors if the stocks they buy become the vehicle for short-term trading profits that in turn weaken the stock?

Consider Primerica Corp., a large financial services holding company that has taken full advantage of Regulation S. In April 1993 the company sold 7 million shares in a Reg-S offering handled by the prestigious Morgan Stanley Group. The company did not at that time inform shareholders of this offering. The market price of Primerica stock at the time was \$46⅛. The Reg-S shares were discounted at \$42¾ to \$43¼ (a very modest discount as these deals go). The day after the offering was completed, the stock fell sharply on trading three times the norm. Now, there can be only one explanation for this activity: The foreign investors were quick to dump the stock by shorting it. A year later

Primerica merged with Travelers Co., and the stock now trades under the Travelers Inc. name. Late in 1994 it was trading at $33 a share.

Any doubts about Reg-S at Primerica/Travelers? Not yet. Not officially. Jamie Dimon, the president of Travelers, told *The Wall Street Journal* that his company would make the Reg-S offering again. "It's fast, efficient, and effective even though it had some negatives to it," he said.

Thomas VanWeelden, president of Allied Waste Industries, which sold $10 million worth of Reg-S convertible debentures—discounted, of course—explained that his company resorted to Reg-S because environmental stocks were out of favor on the Street at the time, while the company was doing quite well. Reg-S seemed to be the only way to reach new investors.

Allied Waste Industries is a solid corporation. But as Reg-S specialist Carol Martino reminds us, many Reg-S companies are money-losing enterprises that are unable to fund their operations or sell their stock in any other way. Very often these companies derive the bulk of their income from Reg-S proceeds—a sure sign of a failing enterprise. Martino says, "A lot of due diligence should be done by people who want to invest in these securities to make sure that they don't end up buying garbage."

How many billions of dollars have how many companies raised through how many Reg-S offerings in the past four years? Since no one keeps score, no one knows. Any number of investment banking firms proselytize for Reg-S business on the sell side, assuring Small-Cap companies that they can raise millions of dollars in less than a month. One respected anaylyst who must remain anonymous makes the educated guess that total Regulation S offerings have amounted to at least 5 percent of all U.S. stock offerings since 1990.

Our favorite freelancer, Walda Walling, is just as busy on this domestic sell side of the Reg-S market as she is on the buy side overseas. Just as she has an ultracozy relationship with Franz Munster, she establishes equally cozy relationships with the CEOs and CFOs of target companies stateside. One such satisfied client, the CEO of a technology company, says, "One important thing about Walda is that unlike Michael Milken, she doesn't take so big a cut of the money that she raises for us. And of course she's much prettier—and more romantic—than Milken." (Walda's 10 percent cut of a deal is the norm for investment banking. Milken often got 30 percent, sometimes as much as 50 percent, depending on the deal.)

Before starting out on her own, Walda worked for several years as a stockbroker and trader for various small securities firms, where she learned to be careful in picking out her companies. Walda's license as a broker was revoked when a company she was working with in the early 1980s got into trouble with the SEC. The firm eventually went out of business. Although Walda was not charged with any wrongdoing, her license was taken from her. She has an uncanny knack for being the first to select a company that needs capital but lacks the resources for raising it, in short, a prime candidate for an infusion of Regulation S capital. It

is not much of an exaggeration to state that Walda's companies are almost wholly undeserving of fresh capital. Less
than a year after their respective financings in 1993, about
five of the fifteen companies Walda helped capitalize had
already ceased trading on the Nasdaq OTC market. That
governing body has certain requirements for listing, such as
adequate capital, and these companies no longer qualified.

At the same time, Walda insists that her clients overseas
make a lot of money on the "special" stocks she deals. "I do
not sell them junk," Walda claims, and this stands to reason.
Investors of this caliber are not likely to put up with a series
of bad stock deals, no matter what Walda's other charms
might be. On the other hand, these investors have so much
money in assets that they need all the available vehicles to
store it. Generally speaking, they're long-term investors. As
I've mentioned, they love the glamorous brand-name
American stocks. (The same holds for small investors, especially in Germany. These individuals love to buy the "local"
mutual funds that invest in the big-time American companies. This is the secret of the staying power of the mutual
funds in countries such as Germany.)

But while the big funds always hold heavily in the big
American stocks, they are ready to move when tantalizing
opportunities arise with Small-Cap companies in the United
States—brought to their attention by Walda often enough.
Sometimes they make a killing in those deals, and sometimes they don't. But the killings outweigh the busts. These
funds might also be able single-handedly to prop up the suspect shares for as long as they need to in order to show good

numbers on their performance charts. It's easy enough to prop the price on a narrow float (such as 3 million to 10 million shares outstanding). Own enough shares and you pretty much control the buying and selling. If there are no sellers, the price doesn't change. So the investment can look okay *on paper*. Meanwhile, Franz Munster and the other mutual fund managers wait for some of Walda's big winners to come along and make up for the losses they'll have to take sooner or later on the bad companies.

Walda makes a couple of million annually from her consulting fees with Franz Munster and other overseas investors on the buy side of Reg-S. She gets another fee from the American companies she brings to the table on the sell side. At the same time she is buying and selling for her own portfolio—through an overseas agent, of course, so that the purchases remain legal. Walda's net worth, most all of it accumulated through four years in the Reg-S trade: more than $20 million.

A Truck Driving Story

Finally, here is the tale of my personal experience with the issue of insider trading. In the spring of 1988 I noticed some unusual trading going on in some stocks that had been mentioned in my *Business Week* column, "Inside Wall Street." This weekly column reports on three or four different situations in the market, usually stocks that the big money managers and investment advisers are buying or selling or considering buying or selling. I try to explain the compelling factors in their thinking. I've always been aware of the impact the column has on the stocks in question. The same holds for stocks mentioned by other columnists and broadcasters: The markets often react. Dan Dorfman's pronouncements are practically guaranteed to elicit powerful trading action.

Nearly one million U.S. copies of *Business Week* are printed at four R. R. Donnelley plants around the country early on Thursday morning, starting at around 2 A.M., and then immediately shipped in order to reach subscribers and newsstands starting on Friday. Therefore, trading on any stock mentioned in "Inside Wall Street" should not be affected until Friday's market—never on Thursday. Just to be certain this wasn't happening, I routinely checked the office computer each Thursday afternoon to see how the stocks I had mentioned for that week were behaving.

As early as 1986 I had noticed some unusual trading on occasion, but it was nothing I would call suspicious. Many Thursdays went by with nothing unusual happening. When trades did catch my attention, there invariably would be another reason behind the buying or selling. Sometimes a company had just held a meeting with analysts. Sometimes the company had just issued an announcement. Sometimes analysts had come out with a new recommendation on a stock—on Tuesday, say, and the impact of those reports was still being felt on Thursday. Suffice it to say that if there was any irregular trading that year, it failed to arouse my suspicion.

In 1987 the situation changed. That spring and summer, before Black Monday in October, my senior editor, Seymour Zucker, and I began to notice with some regularity suspicious price changes on Thursday. On one particular day, March 26, there was heavy Thursday trading in three of the four stocks I had mentioned in the column: Zenith Laboratories, Cadnetix, and Autodesk. Zucker and I spent a couple of weekends in the office tracking the Thursday price changes in the stocks mentioned in my column that year and the year before.

Zucker and William Wolman, *Business Week*'s chief economist, who spearheads the magazine's financial reporting group, promptly apprised the editor in chief, Steve Shepard, of the situation. Following Shepard's review of the matter, the editors moved to solve the problem by tightening security procedures. *Business Week* sharply restricted access to my column by staff members during the editing process and also put in place secret codes and procedures to thwart any opportunity for unauthorized reading of the column in the editorial offices as well as in the printing plants. The magazine also reduced from 600 to 20 the number of copies distributed in the McGraw-Hill building before the market's close on Thursday. And the page containing my column was even pulled from those copies before they were distributed.

The tightened security appeared to work. We noticed a considerable abatement in Thursday price spikes. But not for long. In the spring of 1988, with the stock market in a vigorously upbeat spirit after the gigantic crash in October, Zucker and I again spotted signs of Thursday activity. Zucker, one of the brightest editors of the magazine—and one of the most intense—couldn't believe that there could be suspicious Thursday trades again. Extremely worried, Zucker asked me to check my sources on some of my stories to find out what was going on. Zucker told Wolman that *Business Week* had to take added security measures to plug possible leaks—if any—at the magazine. On April 18 five stocks mentioned in the column jumped considerably. Such suspicious trading was sporadic and irregular, but it was sufficient to attract the attention this time of the "Stock Watch" department of the New York Stock Exchange. This oversight group began its own inquiry in May 1988, looking into the trading of twenty stocks by twenty-six Big Board member firms. Unaware of that development, *Business Week* in early July retained the investigative firm Kroll Associates to start its own investigation. Our goal: To submit the findings to the SEC and other law enforcement agencies.

Predictably, journalists also started noticing Thursday spikes. Among them was the budding financial writer Bryan Burrough, who was then working for the *Professional Investor Report* (*PIR*), a Dow Jones & Co. news wire service. Burrough, who has since become famous as the co-author of *Barbarians at the Gate*, was tipped off by an investor that some illegal trading was going on in connection with the "Inside Wall Street" column in *Business Week*. Burrough and the investor arranged a clandestine meeting in a cemetery in Rhode Island. Burrough broke the story on the *PIR* news wire, and newspapers around the country immediately picked it up on July 21. On Friday, July 22, the day after the Burrough story, *The Wall Street Journal* published the PIR report.

The one-day price Thursday jumps ranged from 5 to 26 percent, and the volume increases ranged from 10 to as high as 2,000 percent. In all, the Thursday trading on the twenty stocks yielded potential profits of about $2.4 million. Burrough reported those figures. The same day the SEC contacted *Business Week*, which fully cooperated with the agency and the U.S. attorney's office in the investigation.

In the end, investigations by the SEC, the New York Stock Exchange, the American Stock Exchange, and the National Association of Securities Dealers turned up evidence of questionable trading in stocks mentioned in my column at some two dozen brokerage firms. Although the financial stakes were much lower, the combined investigations were the most wide-ranging on the issue of insider trading since the blockbusters that brought Ivan Boesky and Michael Milken to justice.

The evidence pointed to several loose networks of brokers and clients on the East Coast and the West Coast, a few of whom appeared to have made a killing. These enterprising brokers had been front-running the column by obtaining bootlegged copies on Thursday and trading on that day in anticipation of "tomorrow's" column. Then, when the market for the stocks reacted up or down on Friday, as it often did in "response" to my column, the front-runners were already positioned to take advantage of the spike or dip.

These brokers' networks began to unravel. Specifically, the compliance unit at Merrill Lynch ordered computer runs on the twenty stocks that seemed to have attracted the most attention. Within hours a suspicious trading pattern was revealed in the personal account of one broker in Merrill Lynch's New London, Connecticut, office. His name was William Dillon.

Merrill Lynch called the SEC, which immediately confronted Dillon with evidence of what amounted to his infallibility in "predicting" with his trades on Thursday what would appear in my column on Friday.

Dillon initially claimed that he picked up tips in casual restaurant conversations with employees of R. R. Donnelley, one of our printers. Finally he spilled the beans on his insider trading scheme and entered a plea agreement involving two counts of fraud. In exchange, he pointed the finger at two other traders: Brad Libera, who executed a total of sixty-five Thursday trades involving the column's stocks in 1987 and netted about $95,000, and a friend of Libera's, Francis Sablone, a lawyer who made fifty-seven trades and netted about $36,000. As a result of Dillon's testimony, both were convicted by a jury in the U.S. district court in Connecticut for conspiracy and insider trading and were sentenced to probated sentences.

Although I was upset when I found out what had been going on, I did get a chuckle out of how Dillon had set up the scheme. At seven-thirty on Thursday mornings, William Sady, an assistant pressman who worked the night shift at the Donnelley plant in Old Saybrook, would enter Pat's Kountry Kitchen, a popular diner in the little town, carrying with him a copy of that day's *Wall Street Journal*. He was met by a man wearing the dark suit emblematic of a white-collar professional. This was William Dillon. The two

conspirators ate breakfast and engaged in animated conversation. Then each went his separate way, but with the stockbroker Dillon carrying the copy of *The Wall Street Journal.*
And inside the newspaper was an unbound copy of *Business
Week,* which the printer, Sady, had had no trouble getting
hot off the press.

Dillon paid Sady $30, plus he picked up the check at Pat's
Kountry Kitchen. Later that morning Dillon began entering
1,000- to 3,000-share orders for the stocks mentioned in
"Inside Wall Street." In a good week Dillon would make several thousand dollars for his personal account. Then he was
caught. Sady lost his job.

Unknown to Dillon and Sady, a similar scheme was being
transacted by another broker and another Donnelley
employee at the Old Saybrook plant, and this guy was even
more enterprising than Dillon had been. One Thursday
morning at six o'clock he had positioned his car—a blue
Chevy, as I recall—along Interstate 95 somewhere in
Connecticut. He parked the car, put up the hood as a way
to fake a breakdown, and waited. Of course this wasn't just
a shot in the dark. Like any good broker, he had done his
research. He knew that the delivery truck from the
Donnelley printing plant in Old Saybrook would be along in
about twenty minutes. When this stockbroker saw the truck
carrying the copies of *Business Week* approaching, he waved
for assistance. The driver obligingly stopped. The stockbroker approached and asked the driver to sell him a copy of
the magazine for $100. He explained that this was of the
utmost importance; he had to get an early copy.

Strange, muttered the driver, but still he reached for a copy of the magazine that he had taken earlier from the plant.

"By the way," said the broker, "could we do this same thing next week and perhaps every Thursday?"

The truck driver saw no reason why he should agree to this proposition, and he refused the money.

The driver then told his boss about his unscheduled delivery by the side of Interstate 95, and he was perhaps fortunate that his superior let him off with a reprimand. Of course, every Thursday morning in the future he glanced at the old rendezvous spot, but he never saw the early-rising stockbroker again. Nor did the SEC catch the man.

Out on the West Coast one source of illicit trading was unmasked in late June 1988 by Bradley C. Weddon, the manager of Prudential's Anaheim office, who noticed that one of his brokers, Brian Callahan, placed sizable orders early on most Thursday mornings. The orders were often for stocks that had been mentioned in my column. Eventually identified as the source of Callahan's information was William Jackson, a quality-control worker at the Donnelley plant in Torrance, California. Jackson had telephoned trading orders to Callahan, who had then traded the stocks for other customer accounts. Prudential fired Callahan, and Donnelley dismissed Jackson.

In all, about fifteen brokers and clients have been charged with insider trading in connection with my column. The courts held in several of these cases that "Inside Wall Street" was indeed "material, nonpublic information," mainly because McGraw-Hill and Donnelley imposed a confidentiality policy forbidding release of the information prior to Friday.

One case that was personally sad for me and many other employees at *Business Week* was the related conviction in April 1989 of Rudy Ruderman, a veteran radioman who was the magazine's broadcaster. Rudy, sixty-two years old, was a gentle, jovial well-liked pro who would never be suspected of wrongdoing, but he admitted to making fifty illegal transactions that were based on the stocks mentioned in my column, which he had obtained from proofs to which he had official access. Ironically, he was allowed access to the proofs to precisely prevent him from inadvertently mentioning in his radio broadcasts the stocks mentioned in my column. Rudy maintained that he didn't realize his actions constituted insider trading. He was charged with two counts of mail fraud in connection with insider trading, and he went to jail for six months.

To my knowledge, no one suspected me of instigating any of the schemes that revolved around "Inside Wall Street." However, many people assume that I have a bulging portfolio of "tipped" stocks. They assume that I use the information, rumor, and innuendo I unearth in my research (much of it "insidy," without a doubt) and the news I "create" in my column to make a fortune. I've been accused of running with the bulls, just as Dorfman is sometimes accused of befriending too many short sellers. But the truth of the matter is, I don't own or trade in any stocks or any securities. The only stock I own is McGraw-Hill, and I never write about McGraw-Hill. *Business Week* has a rigid ethics policy on securities ownership and trading to guard against conflict of interest among its staff writers and editors. But, the temptation and the *danger* of front-running is indeed enormous. It was for R. Foster Winans in 1985. One of several *Wall Street Journal* staffers who wrote the "Heard on the Street" column (the one I worked on when I was at the *Journal* in the 1970s), Winans was convicted of "misappropriating" inside information, fined $5,000, and sentenced to a year in jail.

Epilogue

T hose were the days, my friends, we thought they'd never end. ..." And they haven't. The good times continue to roll, with only a hint of caution all around. The allure of Wall Street and the money to be made there is an intoxicating mistress that is hard to resist. After all, Wall Street's sole function is to produce money.

The Street is the bastion of capitalism, and as such is endowed with an almost exclusive license to print money. It is a club with its own language, distinct mode of thinking, and mysterious *modus operandi*. Its methods are steeped in secrecy, and its focus is myopic: Wall Street's interest is only Wall Street. It is where some of the brightest and smartest minds congregate. But it's also where arrogance and indifference thrive: a perfect breeding ground for incestuous and illicit dealings among its daring and incorrigible cast of characters.

I am certain that I have only scratched the very surface of the vast fertile field of secrets of the Street. Many more are buried there that are yet unknown and untold. Meanwhile, privileged and inside information will continue to be dealt like playing cards, and secrets will be the ace in the hole.